COMMON CORE CLINICS

Grade 4

Mathematics

Number and Operations—Fractions

Common Core Clinics, Mathematics, Number and Operations—Fractions, Grade 4
OT311 / 403NA

ISBN: 978-0-7836-8491-8

Author: Ann Petroni-McMullen

With special thanks to mathematics consultants:
Debra Harley, Director of Math/Science K–12, East Meadow School District
Allan Brimer, Math Specialist, New Visions School, Freeport School District
Cover Image: © herreid/Veer

Triumph Learning® 136 Madison Avenue, 7th Floor, New York, NY 10016

Printed in the United States of America.
10 9 8 7 6 5 4 3 2

ALL ABOUT YOUR BOOK

COMMON CORE CLINICS MATH will help you with key concepts.

A **Key Words** box introduces new math words. An **Example** shows you how to solve problems in the lesson.

Each lesson has **Guided Practice**. Hints called **THINK** and **REMEMBER** help you work through the problem.

There are two pages of **Independent Practice** with problems for you to solve on your own. You will also solve some **Word Problems**.

At the back of your book, there is a **Glossary** and **Math Tools** that will help you work out problems.

Number and Operations–Fractions

Common Core State Standards

1 Equivalent Fractions

Key Words

denominator
equivalent fractions
fraction
numerator

A **fraction** is a number that names equal parts of a whole or equal parts of a group. The **numerator** of a fraction is the top number. It tells how many equal parts are represented by the fraction. The **denominator** is the bottom number. It tells the number of equal parts into which the whole or the group is divided.

Equivalent fractions name the same amount but have different numerators and denominators. To find equivalent fractions, multiply the numerator and the denominator by the same number. When you multiply the numerator and denominator by the same number, you are multiplying the fraction by 1. For example, $\frac{2}{2} = 1$ and $\frac{8}{8} = 1$.

Example

Write two fractions that are equivalent to $\frac{2}{3}$.

Multiply the numerator and the denominator by the same number. Use 2.

$$\frac{2}{3} = \frac{2 \times \mathbf{2}}{3 \times \mathbf{2}}$$
$$= \frac{4}{6}$$

$\frac{1}{3}$	$\frac{1}{3}$	$\frac{1}{3}$

$\frac{1}{6}$	$\frac{1}{6}$	$\frac{1}{6}$	$\frac{1}{6}$	$\frac{1}{6}$	$\frac{1}{6}$

You can use fraction models to see that $\frac{2}{3} = \frac{4}{6}$.

For $\frac{2}{3}$, 2 out of 3 parts are shaded. That model has fewer parts and the parts are larger.

For $\frac{4}{6}$, 4 out of 6 parts are shaded. That model has more parts and the parts are smaller.

The models are the same size and the same amount of each model is shaded. This shows that the fractions $\frac{2}{3}$ and $\frac{4}{6}$ are equivalent.

RELATE

How do the denominators of two equivalent fractions compare with each other? How do the numerators of two equivalent fractions compare with each other? Explain.

Guided Practice

1 Is $\frac{7}{10}$ equivalent to $\frac{5}{6}$?

Step 1 Use fraction models to represent each fraction. Be sure the models are aligned to the same whole.

$\frac{1}{10}$	$\frac{1}{10}$	$\frac{1}{10}$	$\frac{1}{10}$	$\frac{1}{10}$	$\frac{1}{10}$	$\frac{1}{10}$	$\frac{1}{10}$	$\frac{1}{10}$	$\frac{1}{10}$

$\frac{1}{6}$	$\frac{1}{6}$	$\frac{1}{6}$	$\frac{1}{6}$	$\frac{1}{6}$	$\frac{1}{6}$

Step 2 Look at the fraction models.

Do the fractions show the same amount? _______

Is $\frac{7}{10}$ equivalent to $\frac{5}{6}$? _______

THINK

Is the amount shaded to represent $\frac{5}{6}$ the same as the amount shaded to represent $\frac{7}{10}$?

2 What fraction with a denominator of 8 is equivalent to $\frac{1}{2}$?

$\frac{1}{2} = \frac{?}{8}$

Step 1 Find the number that 2 is multiplied by to get 8.

Find the missing factor: $2 \times$ _______ $= 8$

Step 2 Use the factor to find the missing numerator.

$$\frac{1}{2} = \frac{1 \times \square}{2 \times \square} = \frac{\square}{8}$$

$\frac{1}{2} = \frac{\square}{8}$

REMEMBER

To find equivalent fractions, you can multiply the numerator and the denominator by the same number.

Independent Practice

1. Why can you multiply the numerator and the denominator of a fraction by the same number to write an equivalent fraction?

____

____

2. If two fractions are equivalent, what must be true about models for the fractions?

____

____

Ask Yourself

How can I use fraction models to help me decide if the fractions are equivalent?

Find a fraction that is equivalent to each fraction.

3. $\frac{1}{3}$ ______ 4. $\frac{1}{2}$ ______ 5. $\frac{2}{5}$ ______

6. $\frac{1}{4}$ ______ 7. $\frac{3}{4}$ ______ 8. $\frac{3}{5}$ ______

Decide whether the fractions are equivalent. Write *yes* or *no*.

9. $\frac{3}{4}$ and $\frac{3}{6}$ ______ 10. $\frac{1}{3}$ and $\frac{4}{12}$ ______

11. $\frac{1}{2}$ and $\frac{5}{10}$ ______ 12. $\frac{4}{5}$ and $\frac{5}{8}$ ______

13. $\frac{2}{5}$ and $\frac{4}{10}$ ______ 14. $\frac{1}{4}$ and $\frac{3}{12}$ ______

15. $\frac{3}{5}$ and $\frac{1}{2}$ ______ 16. $\frac{4}{8}$ and $\frac{8}{12}$ ______

17. A pizza is cut into 8 equal slices. Dennis eats $\frac{1}{4}$ of the pizza, and Enid eats $\frac{2}{8}$ of the pizza. Did they eat the same amount of pizza? Explain.

____

Complete each equivalent fraction.

18. $\frac{1}{2} = \frac{\square}{6}$

19. $\frac{5}{\square} = \frac{10}{12}$

20. $\frac{3}{4} = \frac{6}{\square}$

21. $\frac{\square}{4} = \frac{3}{12}$

22. $\frac{3}{\square} = \frac{30}{100}$

23. $\frac{2}{6} = \frac{\square}{3}$

24. $\frac{1}{5} = \frac{20}{\square}$

25. $\frac{1}{4} = \frac{\square}{8}$

26. $\frac{1}{\square} = \frac{5}{10}$

27. $\frac{\square}{6} = \frac{2}{3}$

28. $\frac{4}{5} = \frac{\square}{10}$

29. $\frac{6}{\square} = \frac{1}{2}$

Solve each problem.

30. Camille makes a juice blend using $\frac{1}{2}$ cup of orange juice and $\frac{3}{8}$ cup of pineapple juice. Does she use the same amount of orange juice and pineapple juice? Explain.

____

31. Marshall says that $\frac{3}{4}$ and $\frac{3}{8}$ are equivalent fractions. Is he correct? How do you know?

____

32. Wanda and Casey each write a fraction. Wanda's fraction has a denominator of 10. Casey's fraction also has a denominator of 10. What must be true about the numerators for the fractions to be equivalent fractions?

____

2 Mixed Numbers and Improper Fractions

Key Words

improper fraction
mixed number

When the numerator of a fraction is equal to or greater than the denominator of the fraction, the number is called an **improper fraction**. You can rename an improper fraction as a mixed number or as a whole number. A **mixed number** has a whole number part and a fraction part.

Example

Write $\frac{11}{4}$ as a mixed number.

Use fraction models to show $\frac{11}{4}$.

Divide the models into fourths. Shade 11 fourths.

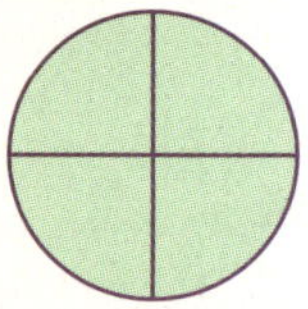

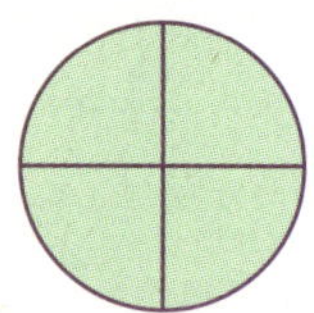

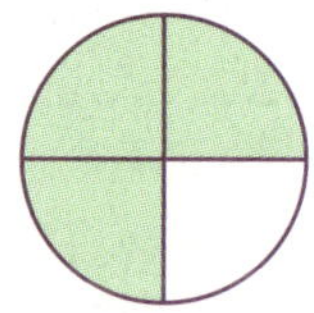

2 wholes are shaded, so the whole-number part of the mixed number is 2.
3 out of 4 sections are shaded, so the fraction part is $\frac{3}{4}$.

You can also divide to write the mixed number.
Divide the numerator by the denominator.

$$\begin{array}{r} 2 \text{ R}3 \\ \text{denominator} \rightarrow 4\overline{)11} \leftarrow \text{numerator} \\ \underline{-8} \\ 3 \leftarrow \text{number of fourths left over} \end{array}$$

Write the quotient as the whole-number part. Then write the remainder as the numerator and the divisor as the denominator for the fraction part.

$\frac{11}{4} = 2\frac{3}{4}$

EXPLAIN

What whole number is equivalent to $\frac{8}{8}$? Explain.

Guided Practice

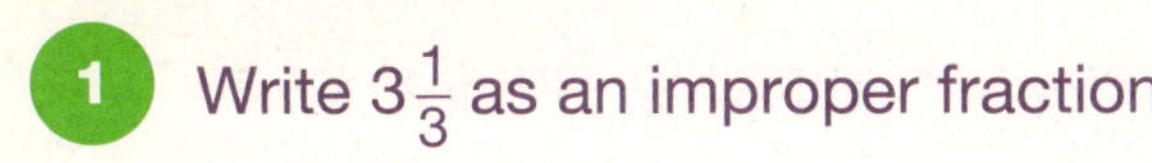

1 Write $3\frac{1}{3}$ as an improper fraction.

Step 1 Use models to show $3\frac{1}{3}$.

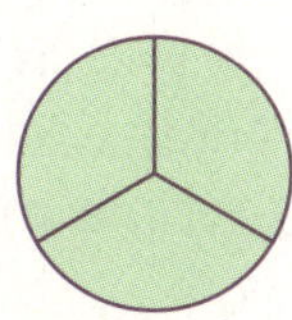
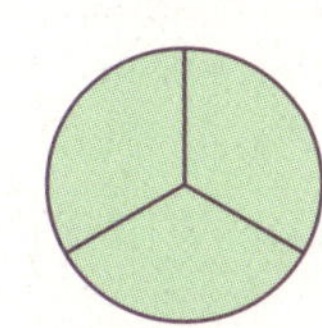
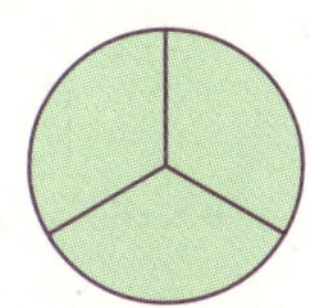
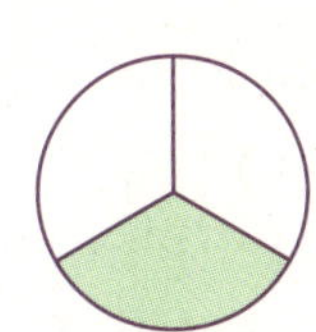

REMEMBER
The number of shaded parts in a fraction is the numerator. The number of equal parts is the denominator.

Step 2 Write the improper fraction.

The total number of shaded parts is ______.

The numerator is ______. The denominator is ______.

The improper fraction is ______.

$3\frac{1}{3}$ = ______

2 Write a mixed number and an improper fraction for the model.

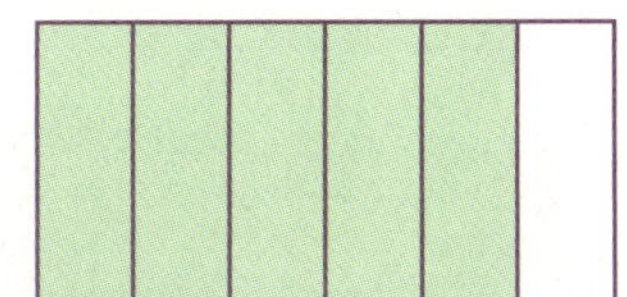

REMEMBER
The denominator is the same for the mixed number and the improper fraction.

Step 1 Write the mixed number.

How many wholes are shaded? ______

What is the numerator of the fraction part? ______

What is the denominator of the fraction part? ______

What is the mixed number? ______

A mixed number for the model is ______.

Step 2 Write the improper fraction.

How many total parts are shaded? ______

The numerator is ______.

The denominator is ______.

The improper fraction is ______.

An improper fraction for the model is ______.

Independent Practice

1. How can models help you rename a mixed number as an improper fraction or an improper fraction as a mixed number?

____

2. How can you tell whether an improper fraction can be written as a whole number or as a mixed number?

____

____

Write an improper fraction and either a whole number or a mixed number for each model.

3. 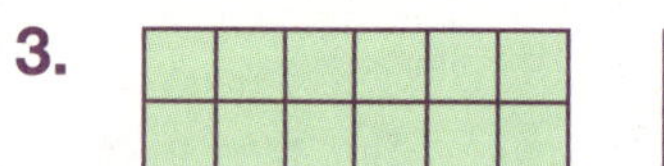 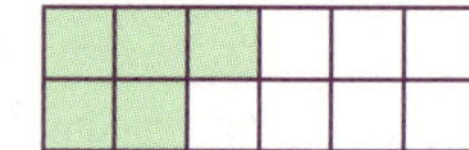

____

4. 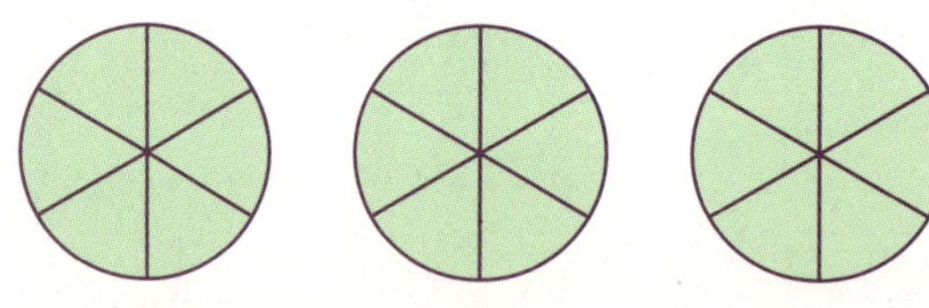

____

5. 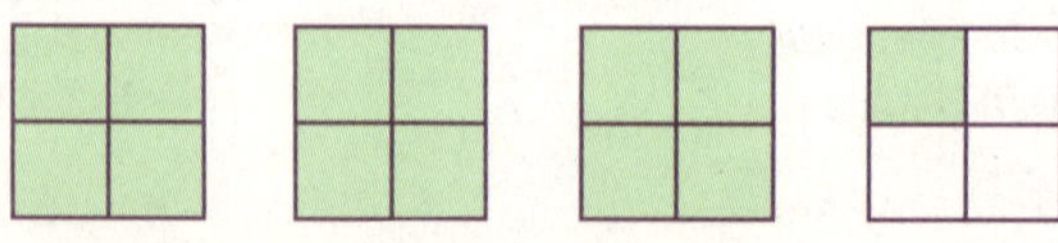

____

6. Each table at a diner seats 4 people. There are $6\frac{3}{4}$ full tables at the diner. How many people are at the diner?

____

Write each improper fraction as either a whole number or a mixed number.

7. $\frac{5}{2}$ ______
8. $\frac{8}{3}$ ______
9. $\frac{25}{8}$ ______
10. $\frac{24}{12}$ ______
11. $\frac{18}{5}$ ______
12. $\frac{31}{10}$ ______
13. $\frac{35}{4}$ ______
14. $\frac{19}{6}$ ______
15. $\frac{20}{4}$ ______

Write each mixed number as an improper fraction.

16. $2\frac{1}{10}$ ______
17. $1\frac{5}{8}$ ______
18. $3\frac{1}{12}$ ______
19. $1\frac{4}{5}$ ______
20. $6\frac{1}{4}$ ______
21. $2\frac{7}{8}$ ______
22. $5\frac{2}{3}$ ______
23. $4\frac{3}{8}$ ______
24. $1\frac{9}{10}$ ______

Solve each problem.

25. Rory has a $\frac{1}{4}$-cup measuring cup. She needs to measure $2\frac{3}{4}$ cups of flour. How many times will she have to fill the measuring cup to measure $2\frac{3}{4}$ cups?

____

26. Ben is making trail mix for 25 people. Each person will get $\frac{1}{8}$-pound of trail mix. How much trail mix does Ben need to make in all? Write your answer as an improper fraction and as a mixed number.

____

27. Cassie uses 6 fabric pieces for each quilt block she makes. Each fabric piece is the same shape and size. She has 15 fabric pieces. How many quilt blocks can Cassie make? Write your answer as an improper fraction and as a mixed number.

____

3 Compare Fractions

Key Words

is equal to
is greater than
is less than

Use these symbols to compare fractions:

$>$ means **is greater than**

$<$ means **is less than**

$=$ means **is equal to**

To compare fractions with the same denominators, compare the numerators. When the denominators are the same, the fraction with the greater numerator is the greater fraction.

$\frac{7}{10} > \frac{4}{10}$

To compare fractions with the same numerators, compare the denominators. When the numerators are the same, the fraction with the greater denominator is the lesser fraction.

$\frac{2}{8} < \frac{2}{3}$

Example

Compare $\frac{2}{5}$ and $\frac{3}{10}$.

Find equivalent fractions.

10 is a multiple of 5, so find a fraction equivalent to $\frac{2}{5}$ with a denominator of 10.

Since $2 \times 5 = 10$, multiply the numerator and the denominator of $\frac{2}{5}$ by 2.

$$\frac{2}{5} = \frac{2 \times 2}{5 \times 2} = \frac{4}{10}$$

Now the fractions have the same denominators, so compare the numerators.

$\frac{\mathbf{4}}{\mathbf{10}} > \frac{\mathbf{3}}{\mathbf{10}}$, so $\frac{2}{5} > \frac{3}{10}$.

Use fraction models to check the comparison. Be sure the models are aligned and represent the same whole.

$\frac{1}{5}$	$\frac{1}{5}$	$\frac{1}{5}$	$\frac{1}{5}$	$\frac{1}{5}$

$\frac{1}{10}$	$\frac{1}{10}$	$\frac{1}{10}$	$\frac{1}{10}$	$\frac{1}{10}$	$\frac{1}{10}$	$\frac{1}{10}$	$\frac{1}{10}$	$\frac{1}{10}$	$\frac{1}{10}$

The bar for $\frac{2}{5}$ is longer than the bar for $\frac{3}{10}$, so $\frac{2}{5} > \frac{3}{10}$.

$\frac{2}{5} > \frac{3}{10}$

GENERALIZE

To compare fractions, the fractions must be part of the same-size whole. Why?

Guided Practice

1 Compare $\frac{1}{3}$ and $\frac{1}{2}$.

Step 1 The fractions have the same numerator. Compare the denominators.

$3 > 2$, so $\frac{1}{3} < \frac{1}{2}$.

REMEMBER
The fraction with the greater denominator is the lesser fraction.

Step 2 Use fraction models to check.

Be sure the wholes are the same size and the ends are lined up.

$\frac{1}{3}$	$\frac{1}{3}$	$\frac{1}{3}$

$\frac{1}{2}$	$\frac{1}{2}$

Step 3 Look at the fraction models.

Which shaded part is longer: $\frac{1}{3}$ or $\frac{1}{2}$? ______

$\frac{1}{3} \bigcirc \frac{1}{2}$

2 Use $\frac{1}{2}$ as a benchmark to compare $\frac{1}{4}$ with $\frac{2}{3}$.

THINK
The numerators are the same. Compare the denominators.

Step 1 Compare $\frac{1}{4}$ to $\frac{1}{2}$.

$4 > 2$, so $\frac{1}{4} \bigcirc \frac{1}{2}$.

Step 2 Compare $\frac{2}{3}$ with $\frac{1}{2}$.

THINK
2 is a multiple of 1, so multiply the numerator and the denominator of $\frac{1}{2}$ by 2.

Write a fraction equivalent to $\frac{1}{2}$ with 2 as a numerator.

$\frac{1}{2} = \frac{1 \times 2}{2 \times 2} = \frac{2}{4}$

Compare the denominators of $\frac{2}{3}$ and $\frac{2}{4}$.

$3 < 4$, so $\frac{2}{3} \bigcirc \frac{2}{4}$. $\frac{2}{4} = \frac{1}{2}$, so $\frac{2}{3} \bigcirc \frac{1}{2}$.

Step 3 Compare $\frac{1}{4}$ and $\frac{2}{3}$.

______ is less than $\frac{1}{2}$, and ______ is greater than $\frac{1}{2}$, so $\frac{1}{4} \bigcirc \frac{2}{3}$.

$\frac{1}{4} \bigcirc \frac{2}{3}$

Independent Practice

1. How do you compare two fractions that have the same denominator?

____

2. If two fractions have the same numerator, how can you compare the fractions? Explain your thinking.

____

Ask Yourself

Do the fractions have the same denominators?

Do the fractions have the same numerators?

How can a model help me compare the fractions?

Compare. Write >, <, or = for each ◯.

3. $\frac{3}{8}$ ◯ $\frac{3}{4}$

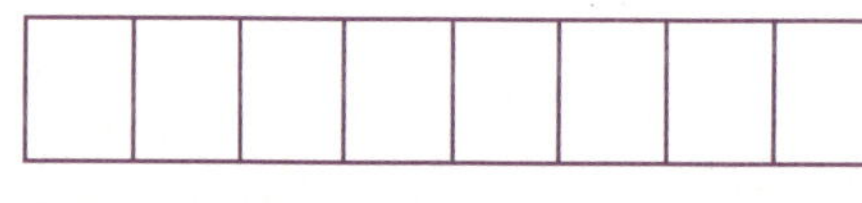

4. $\frac{1}{2}$ ◯ $\frac{3}{6}$

5. $\frac{2}{4}$ ◯ $\frac{4}{5}$

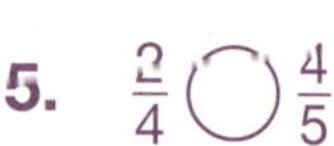

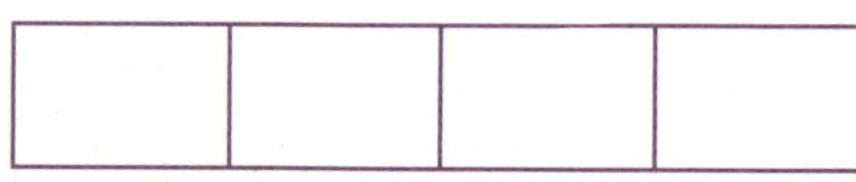

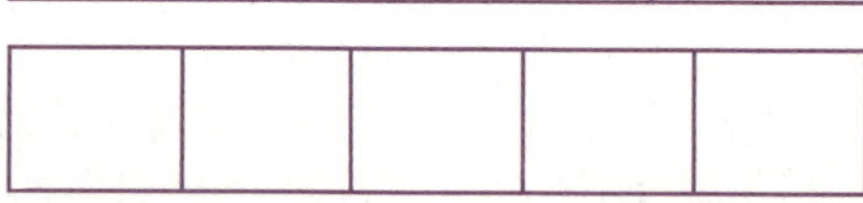

6. $\frac{7}{10}$ ◯ $\frac{5}{8}$

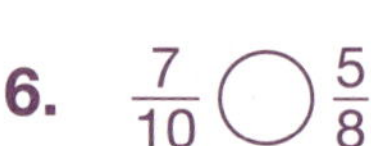

7. $\frac{4}{12}$ ◯ $\frac{2}{6}$

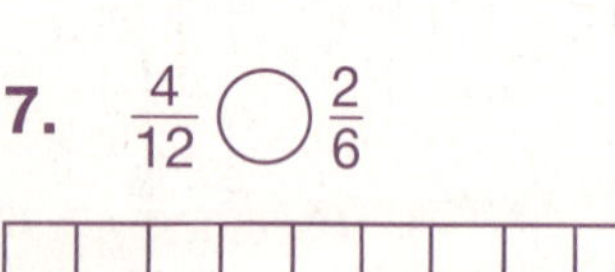

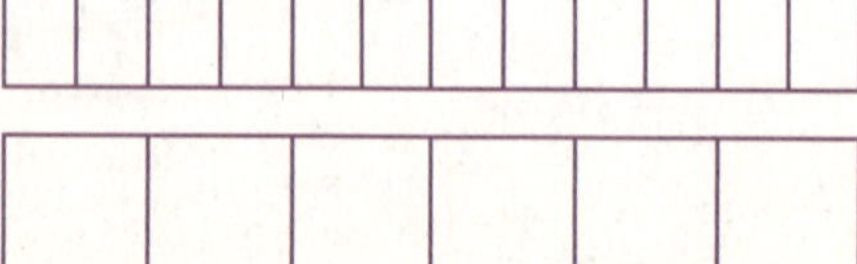

8. $\frac{3}{8}$ ◯ $\frac{2}{3}$

9. Max lives $\frac{7}{8}$ mile from the library and $\frac{3}{4}$ mile from school. Does he live closer to school or to the library? Explain.

____

Compare the fractions. Write $>$, $<$, or $=$.

10. $\frac{2}{5} \bigcirc \frac{4}{5}$

11. $\frac{9}{10} \bigcirc \frac{2}{3}$

12. $\frac{1}{2} \bigcirc \frac{4}{5}$

13. $\frac{3}{4} \bigcirc \frac{5}{12}$

14. $\frac{4}{8} \bigcirc \frac{4}{5}$

15. $\frac{3}{4} \bigcirc \frac{6}{8}$

16. $\frac{7}{8} \bigcirc \frac{7}{10}$

17. $\frac{5}{12} \bigcirc \frac{2}{3}$

18. $\frac{1}{10} \bigcirc \frac{1}{12}$

19. $\frac{2}{3} \bigcirc \frac{5}{6}$

20. $\frac{1}{4} \bigcirc \frac{2}{12}$

21. $\frac{7}{10} \bigcirc \frac{4}{5}$

Solve each problem.

22. Alison bought $\frac{3}{8}$-pound of cashews and $\frac{2}{3}$-pound of almonds to make some trail mix.

a. Did she buy more than $\frac{1}{2}$-pound of cashews? Of almonds? Explain.

____

b. Which did Alison buy more of, cashews or almonds? Explain.

____

23. Ramona and Cicely each had a personal pizza. Ramona cut her pizza into sixths and ate 5 slices. Cicely cut her pizza into fourths and ate 3 slices. Who ate more of the pizza, Ramona or Cicely? Explain.

____

24. Oliver ran $\frac{7}{12}$ mile on Monday. He ran $\frac{9}{10}$ mile on Friday. On which day did he run farther? How do you know?

____

4 Add Fractions

Key Words

addend
like denominators
sum
unit fraction

You can add fractions to join parts that refer to the same whole. The numbers that you add are the **addends**. The answer when you add is the **sum**. Fractions with **like denominators** are fractions that have the same denominator. To add fractions with like denominators, add the numerators and write the sum over the denominator.

Unit fractions are fractions with a numerator of 1.

Example

Waldo sliced a loaf of banana bread into 10 equal slices for a bake sale. He sold 2 of the slices to Carmen and 5 of the slices to Layla. What fraction of the bread did Waldo sell?

Write an addition equation that shows the situation. Let b represent the total number of slices sold.

$$\frac{2}{10} + \frac{5}{10} = b$$

Draw a model to show $\frac{10}{10}$, or 1 whole. Model $\frac{2}{10}$ by shading 2 parts.

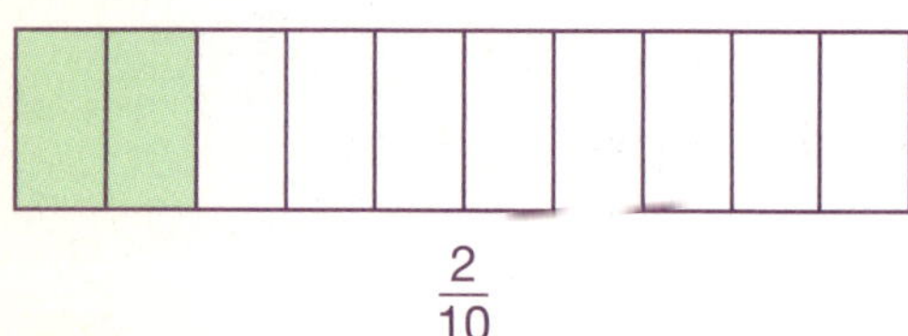

$\frac{2}{10}$

Add $\frac{5}{10}$ by shading 5 more parts.

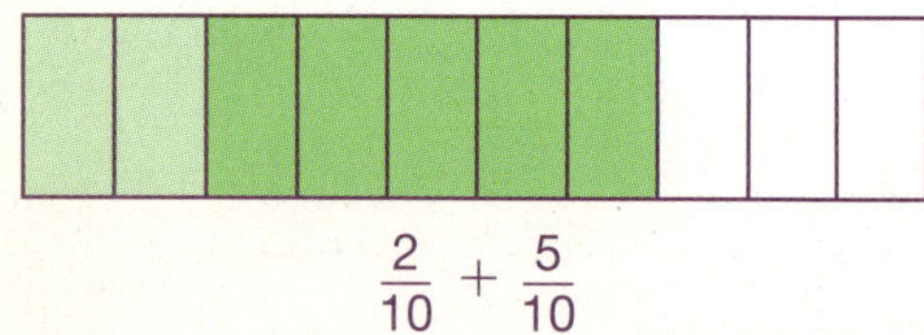

$\frac{2}{10} + \frac{5}{10}$

In all, 7 parts are shaded. So 7 is the numerator. There are 10 equal parts, so the denominator does not change. Write the sum of the numerators over the denominator.

$$\frac{2}{10} + \frac{5}{10} = \frac{2+5}{10} = \frac{7}{10}$$

Waldo sold $\frac{7}{10}$ of the banana bread.

EXPLAIN

Why do you add only the numerators when you add fractions with like denominators?

Guided Practice

1 How can you write $\frac{5}{8}$ as a sum of unit fractions?

Step 1 Draw a model to represent $\frac{8}{8}$, or 1 whole.

Shade the model to show $\frac{5}{8}$.

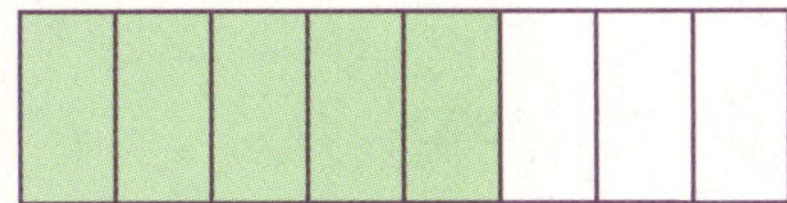

Step 2 Look at the fraction model.

The unit fraction for the model is _______.

How many unit fractions add up to $\frac{5}{8}$? _______

> **THINK**
> A unit fraction has 1 as a numerator.

Step 3 Write $\frac{5}{8}$ as a sum.

_______ + _______ + _______ + _______ + _______ = $\frac{5}{8}$

$\frac{5}{8}$ = _______ + _______ + _______ + _______ + _______

> **REMEMBER**
> When the denominators are the same, add the numerators to add fractions.

2 Find the sum.

$\frac{3}{5} + \frac{3}{5}$

Step 1 The fractions have like denominators.

Add the numerators. Write the sum over the denominator.

$\frac{3}{5} + \frac{3}{5} = \frac{3+3}{5} = \frac{6}{5}$

Step 2 The sum is an improper fraction.

Write the sum as a mixed number.

$\frac{6}{5} = \frac{5}{5} + \frac{1}{5} =$ _______

> **REMEMBER**
> A fraction with a numerator greater than the denominator is an improper fraction.

$\frac{3}{5} + \frac{3}{5} =$ _______

Independent Practice

1. How can you use models to add fractions with like denominators?

____

____

2. How can you use a rule to add fractions with like denominators?

____

____

Ask Yourself

When do I need to write the sum as a whole number or as a mixed number?

Draw a model to find each sum.

3. $\frac{1}{6} + \frac{3}{6} =$ ______

4. $\frac{2}{3} + \frac{2}{3} =$ ______

5. $\frac{3}{10} + \frac{4}{10} =$ ______

6. $\frac{3}{8} + \frac{7}{8} =$ ______

7. Write $\frac{2}{3}$ as a sum of unit fractions. ______________

8. Write $\frac{6}{10}$ as a sum of unit fractions. ______________

9. Melissa walks $\frac{3}{8}$ mile to school in the morning.
She walks the same distance home in the afternoon.
How far does Melissa walk to and from school each day?

____

Find each sum.

10. $\frac{1}{5} + \frac{3}{5} =$ _____

11. $\frac{2}{3} + \frac{1}{3} =$ _____

12. $\frac{2}{10} + \frac{3}{10} =$ _____

13. $\frac{1}{2} + \frac{1}{2} =$ _____

14. $\frac{3}{4} + \frac{2}{4} =$ _____

15. $\frac{2}{6} + \frac{3}{6} =$ _____

16. $\frac{9}{10} + \frac{3}{10} =$ _____

17. $\frac{4}{12} + \frac{5}{12} =$ _____

18. $\frac{4}{5} + \frac{3}{5} =$ _____

19. $\frac{2}{12} + \frac{8}{12} =$ _____

20. $\frac{7}{10} + \frac{1}{10} =$ _____

21. $\frac{6}{8} + \frac{4}{8} =$ _____

Compare. Write <, >, or =.

22. $\frac{2}{6} + \frac{2}{6} \bigcirc \frac{1}{3}$

23. $\frac{3}{12} + \frac{2}{12} \bigcirc \frac{1}{2}$

24. $\frac{1}{4} + \frac{1}{4} \bigcirc \frac{3}{8}$

Solve each problem.

25. Wendy read $\frac{4}{10}$ of a book on Saturday. On Sunday, she read another $\frac{5}{10}$ of the book. How much of the book did Wendy read over the weekend?

____

26. Each lap in a pool is $\frac{1}{12}$ mile. Carl swims 3 laps, rests, and then swims 4 more laps. How far does Carl swim?

____

27. Scott uses $\frac{3}{4}$ cup of white flour, $\frac{3}{4}$ cup of whole-wheat flour, and $\frac{1}{4}$ cup of rye flour to make a loaf of bread. How much flour does Scott use in all?

____

5 Subtract Fractions

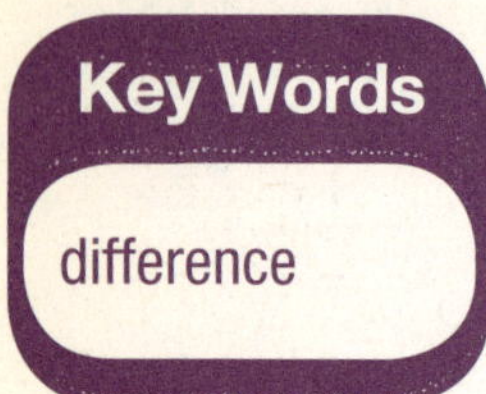

When you subtract fractions, you are removing parts of the whole. The answer when you subtract is the **difference**.

To subtract fractions with like denominators, subtract the numerators and write the difference over the denominator.

Example

Heather walked $\frac{7}{8}$ mile to the park. Jamie walked $\frac{5}{8}$ mile to the park. How much farther did Heather walk to get to the park than Jamie?

Write a subtraction equation that represents the information in the problem. Let w represent how much farther Heather walked.

$$\frac{7}{8} - \frac{5}{8} = w$$

Draw a rectangle to show $\frac{8}{8}$, or 1 whole. Model $\frac{7}{8}$ by shading 7 parts.

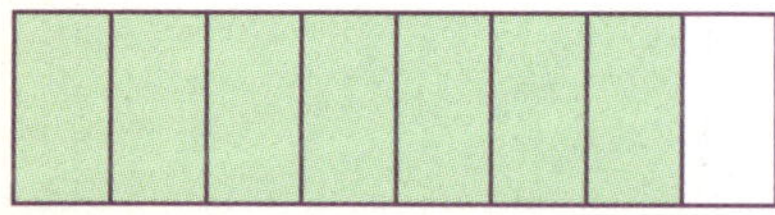

Subtract $\frac{5}{8}$ by crossing out 5 of the shaded parts.

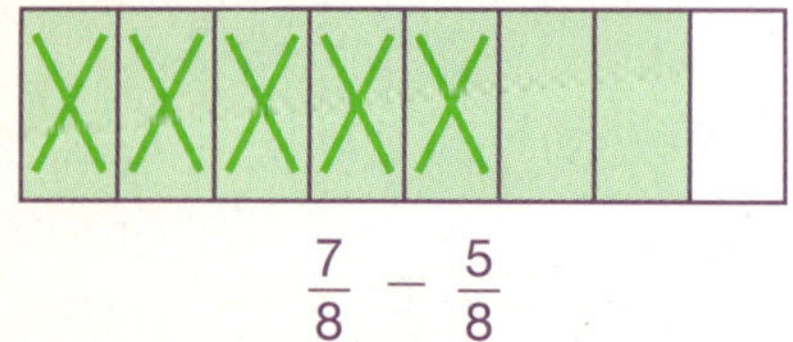

$$\frac{7}{8} - \frac{5}{8}$$

There are 2 parts that are not crossed out. This is the numerator. There are 8 equal parts, so the denominator does not change.

Write the difference of the numerators over the denominator.

$$\frac{7}{8} - \frac{5}{8} = \frac{7-5}{8} = \frac{2}{8}$$

Write an equivalent fraction for the difference. 2 and 8 are multiples of 2. Divide the numerator and the denominator by 2.

$$\frac{2}{8} = \frac{2 \div 2}{8 \div 2} = \frac{1}{4}$$

Heather walked $\frac{2}{8}$ or $\frac{1}{4}$ mile more than Jamie.

DESCRIBE

Why does the denominator stay the same when you subtract fractions with like denominators?

Guided Practice

1 Find the difference.

$\frac{9}{12} - \frac{2}{12}$

Step 1 Draw a model to represent $\frac{12}{12}$, or 1 whole.

Shade the model to show $\frac{9}{12}$.

Step 2 Subtract $\frac{2}{12}$.

Cross out 2 parts of the model.

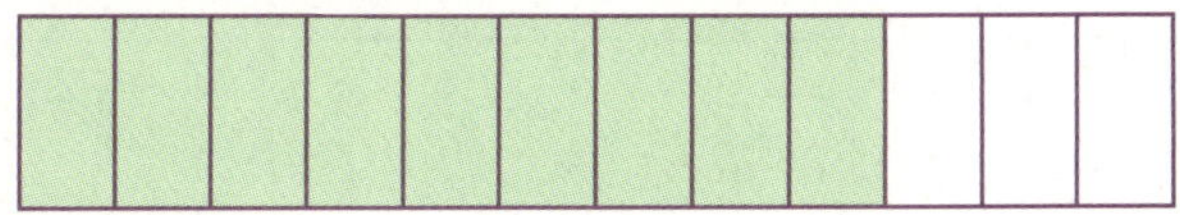

Step 3 Write the difference.

The difference is ______.

$\frac{9}{12} - \frac{2}{12} =$ ______

> **THINK**
> Write the fraction that represents the shaded parts that are not crossed out on the model.

2 Seth took $\frac{5}{6}$ hour to do a science experiment. He took $\frac{2}{6}$ hour to write a report about his experiment. How much longer did Seth take to do the experiment than to write the report?

Step 1 The fractions have like denominators.

Subtract the numerators. Write the difference over the denominator.

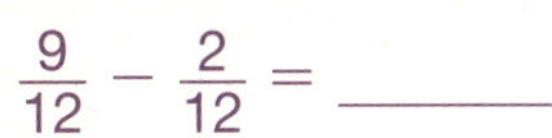

$\frac{5}{6} - \frac{2}{6} = \frac{5-2}{6} = \frac{3}{6}$

Step 2 Write the difference as a fraction equivalent to $\frac{3}{6}$.

$\frac{3}{6} = \frac{3 \div \square}{6 \div \square} = \frac{\square}{\square}$

> **REMEMBER**
> Subtract the lesser fraction from the greater fraction.

> **THINK**
> 3 and 6 are multiples of 3. Divide the numerator and the denominator by 3.

Seth took _____ or _____ hour longer to do the experiment.

Independent Practice

1. How can you use models to subtract fractions with like denominators?

____

____

2. How can you use a rule to subtract fractions with like denominators?

____

____

Ask Yourself

How can I use a model to check the difference?

Draw a model to find each difference.

3. $\frac{5}{8} - \frac{3}{8} =$ ______

4. $\frac{2}{3} - \frac{1}{3} =$ ______

5. $\frac{4}{5} - \frac{1}{5} =$ ______

6. $\frac{9}{10} - \frac{4}{10} =$ ______

7. $\frac{3}{5} - \frac{2}{5} =$ ______

8. $\frac{7}{8} - \frac{3}{8} =$ ______

9. Eric has a board that is $\frac{5}{6}$ yard long. He cuts the board into two pieces. One of the pieces is $\frac{3}{6}$ yard long. How long is the other piece?

____

Find each difference.

10. $\frac{3}{5} - \frac{1}{5} =$ ______

11. $\frac{4}{6} - \frac{1}{6} =$ ______

12. $\frac{8}{10} - \frac{3}{10} =$ ______

13. $\frac{9}{12} - \frac{3}{12} =$ ______

14. $\frac{5}{8} - \frac{2}{8} =$ ______

15. $\frac{6}{12} - \frac{4}{12} =$ ______

16. $\frac{9}{10} - \frac{3}{10} =$ ______

17. $\frac{8}{12} - \frac{1}{12} =$ ______

18. $\frac{1}{2} - \frac{1}{2} =$ ______

19. $\frac{8}{12} - \frac{4}{12} =$ ______

20. $\frac{7}{10} - \frac{1}{10} =$ ______

21. $\frac{6}{8} - \frac{4}{8} =$ ______

Compare. Write <, >, or =.

22. $\frac{5}{8} - \frac{2}{8} \bigcirc \frac{1}{2}$

23. $\frac{10}{12} - \frac{4}{12} \bigcirc \frac{1}{2}$

24. $\frac{5}{6} - \frac{2}{6} \bigcirc \frac{1}{3}$

Solve each problem.

25. Vanessa lives $\frac{7}{10}$ mile from the library. She lives $\frac{3}{10}$ mile from the park. How much closer does she live to the park than to the library?

____

26. A recipe for pumpkin bread calls for $\frac{3}{4}$ teaspoon of cinnamon and $\frac{1}{4}$ teaspoon of ginger. How much more cinnamon than ginger is needed for the recipe?

____

27. Gill bought $\frac{7}{8}$ pound of walnuts. He bought $\frac{2}{8}$ pound less of pecans than he bought of walnuts. How many pounds of nuts did Gill buy in all? Explain how you found your answer.

____

____

6 Add and Subtract Mixed Numbers

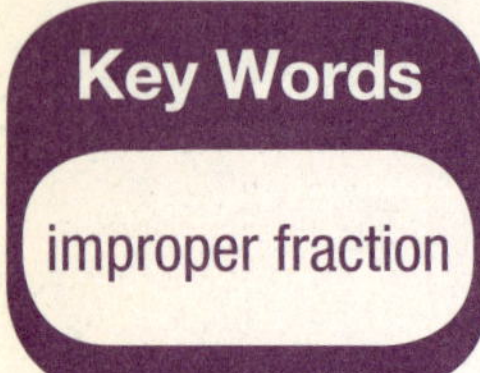

In **improper fractions**, the numerator is greater than or equal to the denominator. You can use equivalent improper fractions to add and subtract mixed numbers. This model shows that a mixed number can be written as an improper fraction.

$$2\frac{3}{5} = 1 + 1 + \frac{3}{5}$$
$$= \frac{5}{5} + \frac{5}{5} + \frac{3}{5}$$
$$= \frac{13}{5}$$

Example

Add: $1\frac{2}{5} + 2\frac{2}{5}$

Write each mixed number as an equivalent improper fraction.

$$1\frac{2}{5} = 1 + \frac{2}{5}$$
$$= \frac{5}{5} + \frac{2}{5}$$
$$= \frac{7}{5}$$

$$2\frac{2}{5} = 1 + 1 + \frac{2}{5}$$
$$= \frac{5}{5} + \frac{5}{5} + \frac{2}{5}$$
$$= \frac{12}{5}$$

Add the fractions.

$$\frac{7}{5} + \frac{12}{5} = \frac{19}{5}$$

Write the sum as a mixed number.

$$\frac{19}{5} = 19 \div 5 = 3 \text{ R}4$$

Write the remainder as a fraction of the denominator.

Write 3 R4 as $3\frac{4}{5}$.

$$1\frac{2}{5} + 2\frac{2}{5} = 3\frac{4}{5}$$

COMPARE

How is adding mixed numbers like adding fractions?

Guided Practice

Find the difference.

$2\frac{5}{8} - 1\frac{2}{8}$

> **THINK**
> Use the denominator of the fraction part of the mixed number as the denominator of the improper fraction.

Step 1 Write $2\frac{5}{8}$ as an improper fraction.

Draw a model.

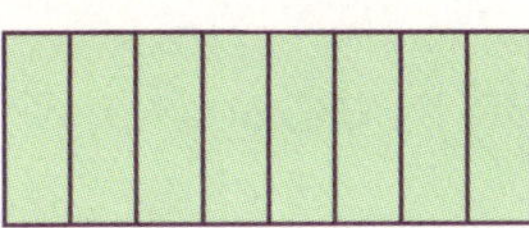
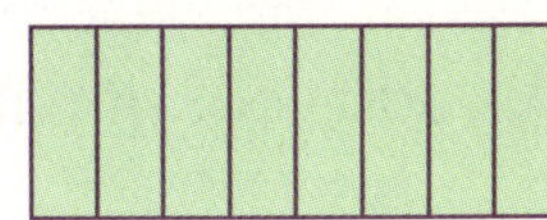
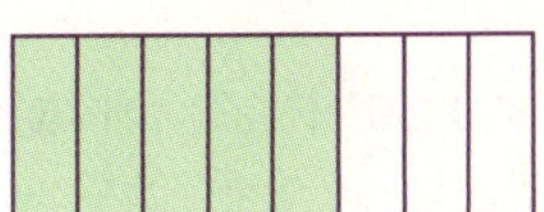

$$2\frac{5}{8} = 1 + 1 + \frac{5}{8}$$
$$= \frac{8}{8} + \frac{8}{8} + \frac{5}{8}$$
$$= \frac{21}{8}$$

Step 2 Write $1\frac{2}{8}$ as an improper fraction.

Draw a model.

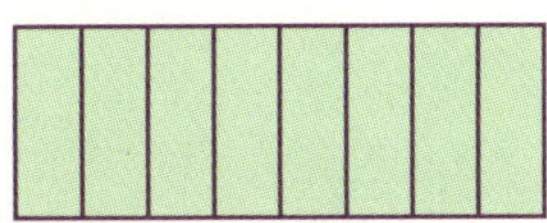

> **REMEMBER**
> Any fraction with the same numerator and denominator is equal to 1.

$$1\frac{2}{8} = 1 + \frac{2}{8}$$
$$= \_\_\_\_\_\_ + \_\_\_\_\_\_$$
$$= \_\_\_\_\_\_$$

Step 3 Subtract the fractions.

$$\frac{21}{8} - \frac{10}{8} = \_\_\_\_\_\_$$

Step 4 Write the difference as a mixed number.

$$\frac{\square}{\square} = \square\frac{\square}{8}$$

> **REMEMBER**
> To write an improper fraction as a mixed number, divide the numerator by the denominator.

$2\frac{5}{8} - 1\frac{2}{8} = \_\_\_\_\_\_$

Independent Practice

1. How is adding or subtracting mixed numbers different from adding or subtracting fractions with like denominators?

____

____

2. How can you use subtraction to check addition with mixed numbers?

____

____

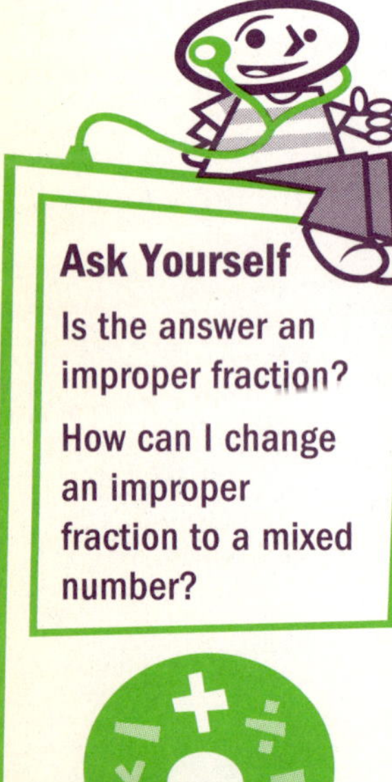

Draw a model. Write each mixed number as an improper fraction.

3. $2\frac{1}{2} =$ ______

4. $1\frac{7}{8} =$ ______

5. $3\frac{3}{5} =$ ______

6. $2\frac{3}{4} =$ ______

Find each sum or difference.

7. $2\frac{1}{2} + 1\frac{1}{2} =$ ______

8. $3\frac{5}{6} - 1\frac{3}{6} =$ ______

9. $1\frac{2}{5} + 1\frac{1}{5} =$ ______

10. $1\frac{7}{8} - 1\frac{3}{8} =$ ______

11. Julius is making a fruit salad. He mixes $1\frac{3}{4}$ cups of grapes with $2\frac{3}{4}$ cups of apple slices. How much fruit salad does Julius make?

____

Find each sum or difference.

12. $2\frac{8}{10} - 1\frac{5}{10} =$ ______

13. $4\frac{3}{6} + 1\frac{2}{6} =$ ______

14. $5\frac{2}{3} - 1\frac{1}{3} =$ ______

15. $3\frac{3}{5} + 2\frac{1}{5} =$ ______

16. $4\frac{6}{8} - 2\frac{4}{8} =$ ______

17. $2\frac{1}{4} + 3\frac{1}{4} =$ ______

18. $4\frac{2}{3} - 1\frac{2}{3} =$ ______

19. $2\frac{5}{12} - 1\frac{1}{12} =$ ______

20. $6\frac{5}{8} - 1\frac{3}{8} =$ ______

21. $5\frac{2}{8} + 2\frac{7}{8} =$ ______

22. $1\frac{3}{5} + 4\frac{2}{5} =$ ______

23. $1\frac{1}{3} + 1\frac{2}{3} + \frac{2}{3} =$ ______

Solve each problem.

24. Mindy feeds her dog $2\frac{3}{4}$ cups of dog food each day. She gives him $1\frac{2}{4}$ cups of dog food in the morning and the rest in the afternoon. How many cups of dog food does Mindy feed her dog in the afternoon?

______

25. Tino ran $3\frac{1}{5}$ miles on Monday and on Wednesday. On Friday, he ran $1\frac{2}{5}$ miles farther than he ran on Monday. How many miles did Tino run in all?

______

26. Corbin works for $15\frac{3}{6}$ hours each week. He has worked $5\frac{4}{6}$ hours each day for two days. How many more hours does Corbin need to work this week?

______

7 Multiply Fractions by Whole Numbers

Key Words

factor
product

When you multiply, the numbers you multiply are called **factors**. The answer is the **product**.

You can use the addition of unit fractions to help you understand how to multiply a fraction by a whole number. For example, multiplying $\frac{1}{5}$ by 4 is the same as adding $\frac{1}{5} + \frac{1}{5} + \frac{1}{5} + \frac{1}{5}$. So $4 \times \frac{1}{5} = \frac{4}{5}$. To multiply a fraction by a whole number, multiply the whole number by the numerator of the fraction. Write the product over the denominator of the fraction.

Example

Olivia and her dad made 6 tacos. Olivia made $\frac{2}{3}$ of the tacos. How many tacos did Olivia make?

Write a multiplication equation to show the situation.
Let t represent the number of tacos Olivia made.

$6 \times \frac{2}{3} = t$

Use fraction models to show 6 groups of $\frac{2}{3}$.
Remember that $\frac{3}{3}$ is equal to 1 whole.

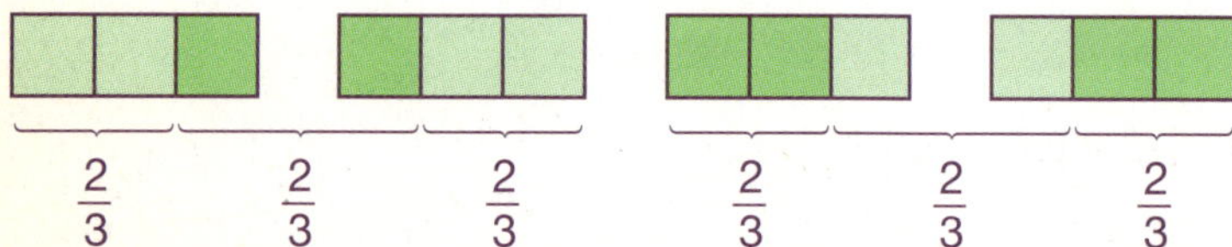

Use repeated addition. Add 6 groups of $\frac{2}{3}$.

$\frac{2}{3} + \frac{2}{3} + \frac{2}{3} + \frac{2}{3} + \frac{2}{3} + \frac{2}{3} = \frac{12}{3} = 4$

Use multiplication. Multiply 6 groups of $\frac{2}{3}$.

$6 \times \frac{2}{3} = \frac{6 \times 2}{3} = \frac{12}{3} = 4$

$6 \times \frac{2}{3} = 4$

Olivia made 4 tacos.

APPLY

How can you write $\frac{12}{3}$ as a product of a whole number and a unit fraction? Use a drawing to support your answer.

Guided Practice

1 Multiply.

$2 \times \frac{3}{4}$

Step 1 Draw 2 groups of $\frac{3}{4}$.

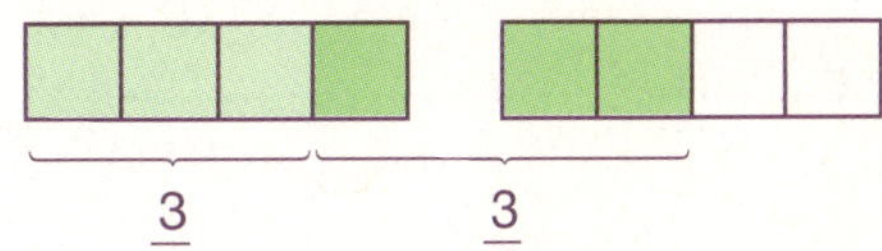

Step 2 Use repeated addition.

Add 2 groups of $\frac{3}{4}$.

$\frac{3}{4} + \frac{3}{4} =$ ______

REMEMBER
The denominator does not change.

Step 3 Use multiplication.

$2 \times \frac{3}{4} = \frac{2 \times 3}{4} =$ ______

Step 4 Write the improper fraction as a mixed number.

$\frac{6}{4} = \square \frac{\square}{4}$

$2 \times \frac{3}{4} =$ ______

2 Vin wants to make 8 smoothies. He uses $\frac{2}{3}$ cup of juice for each smoothie. How much juice does Vince need to make all the smoothies?

Step 1 Write an equation to represent the problem.

Let *j* stand for the juice needed to make all the smoothies.

$8 \times \frac{2}{3} = j$

THINK
Multiply the whole number by the numerator of the fraction. Write the product over the denominator of the fraction.

Step 2 Find the product.

$8 \times \frac{2}{3} = \frac{8 \times 2}{3} = \frac{\square}{3}$

Step 3 Write the product as a mixed number.

$\frac{\square}{3} = \square \frac{\square}{3}$

Vin needs ______ cups of juice.

Independent Practice

1. What is the rule for multiplying a fraction by a whole number?

____

____

2. Explain how you can write $\frac{5}{6}$ as a product of unit fractions. Write $\frac{5}{6}$ as a product of unit fractions.

____

____

Ask Yourself

Which factor tells me the size of each group?

Which factor tells me the number of equal groups?

Write each fraction as a product of unit fractions.

3. $\frac{7}{5}$ = ____________________

4. $\frac{4}{10}$ = ____________________

5. $\frac{8}{12}$ = ____________________

6. $\frac{5}{2}$ = ____________________

Draw a picture to find each product.

7. $6 \times \frac{1}{10}$ = ______

8. $4 \times \frac{2}{5}$ = ______

9. $3 \times \frac{3}{8}$ = ______

10. $2 \times \frac{5}{12}$ = ______

11. A chef uses $\frac{5}{8}$ pound of cheese in each of her special casseroles. She will make 6 casseroles. How much cheese does the chef need?

____

Find each product.

12. $8 \times \frac{1}{3} =$ _______

13. $4 \times \frac{3}{5} =$ _______

14. $2 \times \frac{5}{6} =$ _______

15. $5 \times \frac{1}{2} =$ _______

16. $9 \times \frac{1}{12} =$ _______

17. $6 \times \frac{2}{10} =$ _______

18. $4 \times \frac{9}{10} =$ _______

19. $2 \times \frac{3}{12} =$ _______

20. $7 \times \frac{1}{8} =$ _______

21. $6 \times \frac{4}{6} =$ _______

22. $8 \times \frac{3}{4} =$ _______

23. $5 \times \frac{3}{12} =$ _______

Solve each problem.

24. Kramer bought 16 apples. Of the apples, $\frac{5}{8}$ are red apples. How many red apples did Kramer buy?

____

25. Nora bought a dozen eggs. She used $\frac{3}{4}$ of the eggs to make an omelet. How many eggs did she use in the omelet? (Hint: A dozen is 12.)

____

26. Jordan needs $\frac{7}{12}$ foot of yarn for each border she is putting around a napkin. There are 8 borders. How many feet of yarn does Jordan need in all? Between which two whole numbers is the length?

____

8 Decimals

Key Words

decimal
decimal point

A **decimal** expresses a whole as divided into ten equal parts (tenths), into one hundred equal parts (hundredths), and so on. A **decimal point** separates the whole-number part of the decimal number from the part that is less than 1.

You can use a place-value chart to show the value of each digit in a decimal.

Ones	Decimal Point	Tenths	Hundredths
0	.	4	2

The value of the digit 4 is 4 tenths, or 0.4.

The value of the digit 2 is 2 hundredths, or 0.02.

A fraction with a denominator of 10 or 100 can be written as a decimal.

Example 1

What fraction and decimal does the model show?

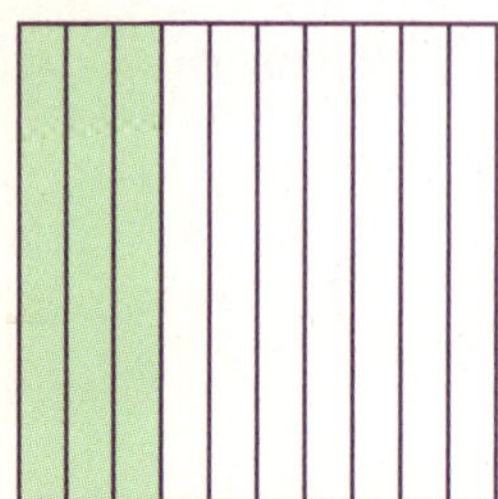

The model has 10 equal parts.

3 of the 10 parts are shaded.

Fraction: $\frac{3}{10}$

Decimal: 0.3

Read: three tenths

The fraction and the decimal name the same amount.

The model shows the fraction $\frac{3}{10}$ and the decimal 0.3.

DEMONSTRATE

How would you shade a model to show $\frac{8}{10}$? What is the decimal for $\frac{8}{10}$?

Guided Practice

1 Write and read the fraction and decimal for the model.

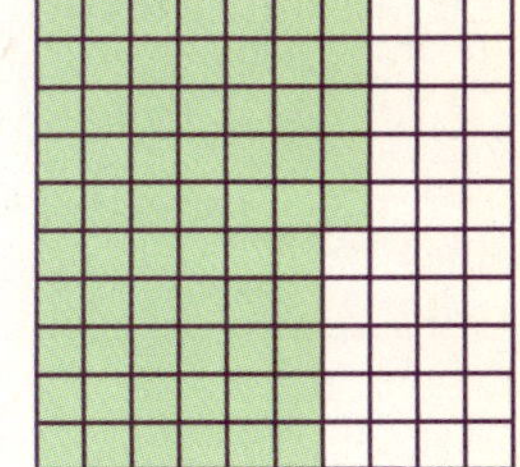

Step 1 Find the number of shaded and unshaded squares.

The model has ________ equal parts.

________ of the total number of squares are shaded.

Step 2 Write and read the fraction and decimal.

Write the fraction: $\frac{\square}{\square}$

Write the decimal: 0.65

Read: sixty-five ____________________

The model shows $\frac{65}{100}$, or ________.

2 Write the decimal for point *M* on the number line.

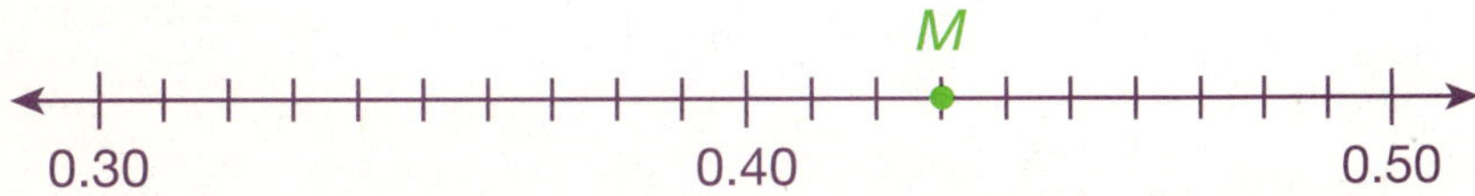

Step 1 Find the number of equal parts that divide the number line.

There are 10 equal parts between 0.40 and 0.50.

Does the number line represent tenths or hundredths? ______________________

Step 2 Count each hundredth until you reach point *M*.

Point *M* is _______ hundredths after 0.40.

The decimal for point *M* is _______.

> **THINK**
> Start counting at 0.40. Each mark represents one hundredth, or 0.01.

Independent Practice

1. How are the models for tenths and hundredths different? How are they alike?

____

____

2. How do you write a fraction in tenths as a decimal? How do you write a fraction in hundredths as a decimal?

____

____

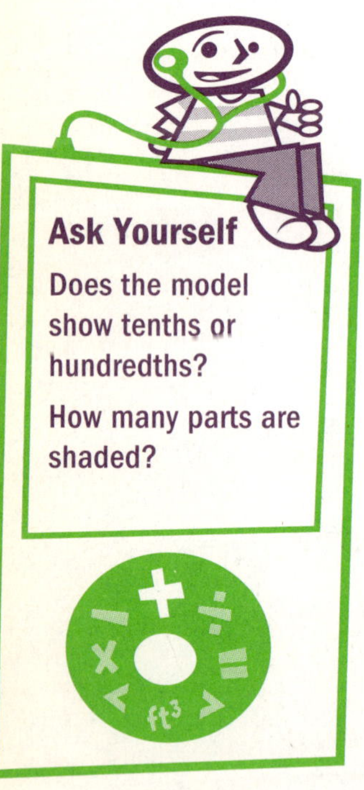

Ask Yourself

Does the model show tenths or hundredths?

How many parts are shaded?

Write a fraction and decimal for each model.

3. 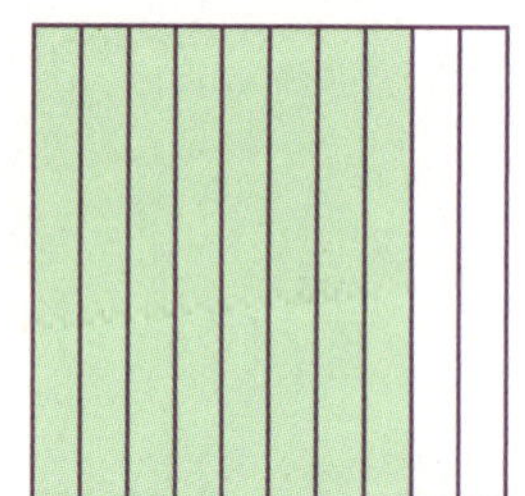

____

4. 

____

5. 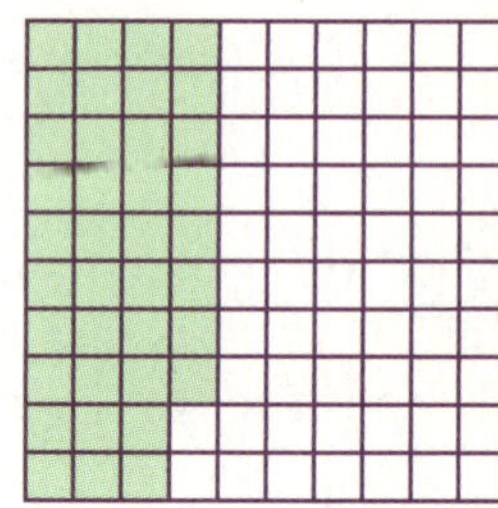

____

6. 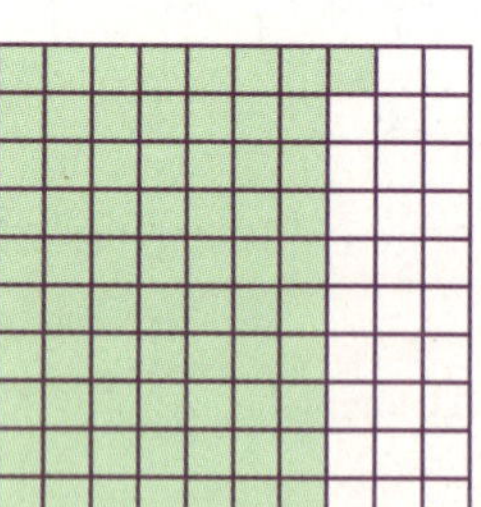

____

7. 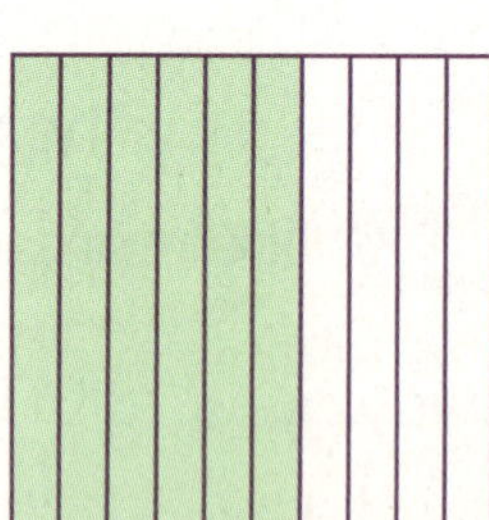

____

8. 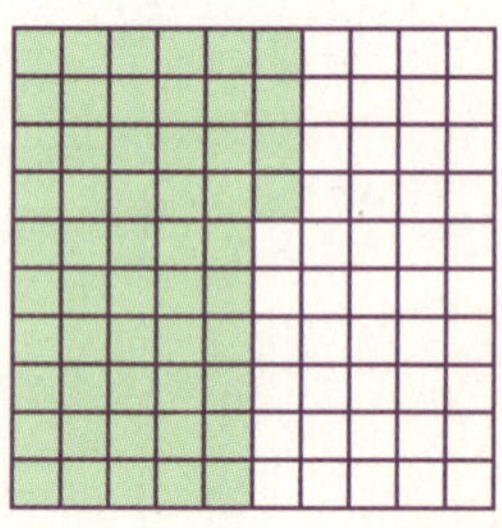

____

9. Dexter made 91 out of 100 hits on a video game. How can he record his number of hits as a fraction and as a decimal?

____

Write the decimal for each point on the number line.

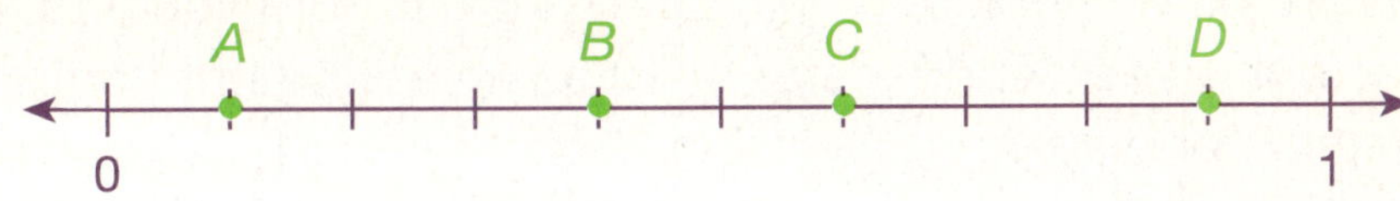

10. Point *A* _____ **11.** Point *B* _____ **12.** Point *C* _____ **13.** Point *D* _____

Write the decimal for each point on the number line.

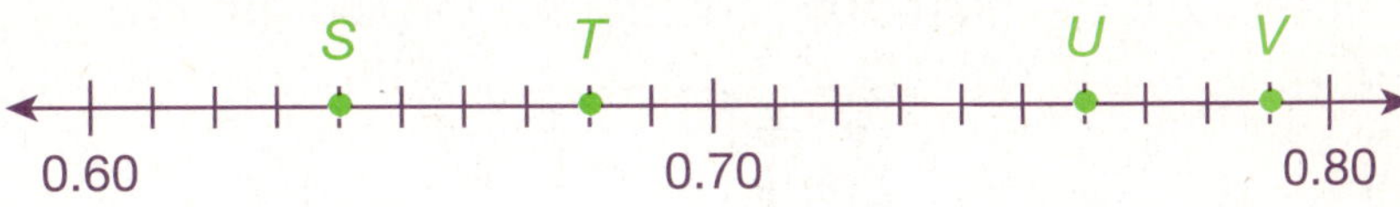

14. Point *S* _____ **15.** Point *T* _____ **16.** Point *U* _____ **17.** Point *V* _____

Write each fraction as a decimal.

18. $\frac{31}{100}$ _____ **19.** $\frac{76}{100}$ _____ **20.** $\frac{5}{10}$ _____ **21.** $\frac{9}{100}$ _____

22. $\frac{69}{100}$ _____ **23.** $\frac{33}{100}$ _____ **24.** $\frac{45}{100}$ _____ **25.** $\frac{8}{10}$ _____

Write each decimal as a fraction.

26. 0.72 _____ **27.** 0.49 _____ **28.** 0.83 _____ **29.** 0.2 _____

Solve each problem.

30. Kimberly walked 0.8 mile to Alissa's house. What is the distance Kimberly walked as a fraction?

____

31. Lizzie made 4 out of 10 free throws at basketball practice. What is 4 out of 10 as a fraction and as a decimal?

____

9 Relate Decimals to Fractions

You can add two fractions when one fraction has a denominator of 10 and the other has a denominator of 100. Before you add, write the fraction with a denominator of 10 as an equivalent fraction with a denominator of 100.

Example

Add: $\frac{4}{10} + \frac{7}{100}$

To add the fractions, they must have the same denominators.

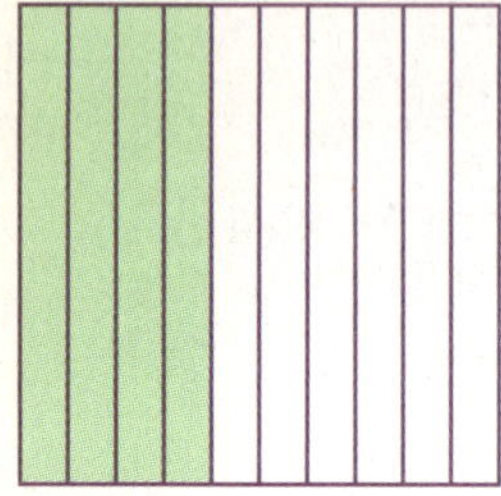

$0.4 = \frac{4}{10}$

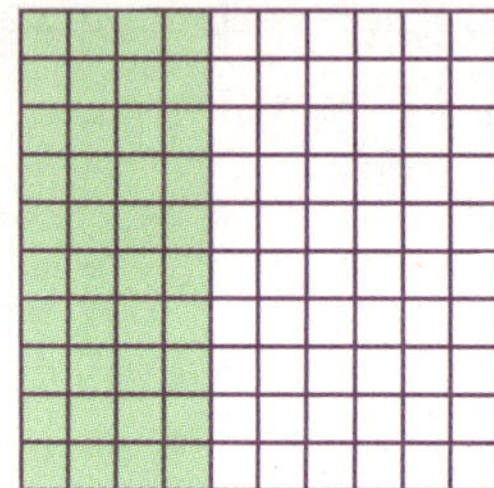

$0.40 = \frac{40}{100}$

Both models show the same part of the whole. They name the same amount.

So $\frac{4}{10}$ and $\frac{40}{100}$ are equivalent fractions: $\frac{4}{10} = \frac{40}{100}$.

You can also multiply the numerator and denominator of $\frac{4}{10}$ by 10 to find the equivalent fractions.

$$\frac{4}{10} = \frac{4 \times \mathbf{10}}{10 \times \mathbf{10}} = \frac{40}{100}$$

Write the addition problem using the equivalent fractions and add.

$$\frac{4}{10} + \frac{7}{100} = \frac{40}{100} + \frac{7}{100}$$

Add the fractions with like denominators.

You can look back at the model for $\frac{40}{100}$ and shade an additional $\frac{7}{100}$.

You can also use the rule for adding fractions with like denominators. Add the numerators, and write the sum over the same denominator.

$$\frac{40}{100} + \frac{7}{100} = \frac{40 + 7}{100} = \frac{47}{100}$$

$\frac{4}{10} + \frac{7}{100} = \frac{47}{100}$

GENERALIZE

Why do the denominators have to be the same to add two fractions?

Guided Practice

1 What fraction with a denominator of 100 is equivalent to $\frac{6}{10}$?

Step 1 Find the number that 10 is multiplied by to get a denominator of 100.

Find the missing factor: $10 \times 10 = 100$

Step 2 Find the numerator of the fraction.

$$\frac{6}{10} = \frac{6 \times \square}{10 \times \square} = \frac{\square}{100}$$

$$\frac{6}{10} = \frac{\square}{100}$$

REMEMBER
To find equivalent fractions, multiply the numerator and the denominator by the same number.

2 Find the sum.

$$\frac{39}{100} + \frac{2}{10}$$

Step 1 Write an equivalent fraction for $\frac{2}{10}$ with a denominator of 100.

To write $\frac{2}{10}$ with a denominator of 100, multiply the numerator and the denominator of $\frac{2}{10}$ by _____.

$$\frac{2}{10} = \frac{2 \times \square}{10 \times \square} = \frac{\square}{\square}$$

THINK
The denominators are different. They must be the same to add the fractions.

Step 2 Write the sum using the equivalent fraction.

$$\frac{39}{100} + \frac{2}{10} = \frac{39}{100} + \frac{\square}{\square}$$

THINK
Replace the addend $\frac{2}{10}$ with the fraction equivalent to $\frac{2}{10}$.

Step 3 Add the fractions with the like denominators.

$$\frac{39}{100} + \frac{\square}{\square} = \frac{39 + \square}{100}$$

$$= \frac{\square}{\square}$$

$$\frac{39}{100} + \frac{2}{10} = \underline{\qquad\qquad}$$

REMEMBER
Add the numerators, and write the sum over the denominator.

Independent Practice

1. Explain how to add a fraction with a denominator of 10 to a fraction with a denominator of 100.

____

2. Can you always write an equivalent fraction with a denominator of 100 for a fraction with a denominator of 10? Why or why not?

____

Write an equivalent fraction with a denominator of 100 for each fraction.

3. $\frac{1}{10}$ ______ 4. $\frac{7}{10}$ ______ 5. $\frac{9}{10}$ ______

Ask Yourself

Which addend must be replaced with an equivalent fraction to add?

Find the sum.

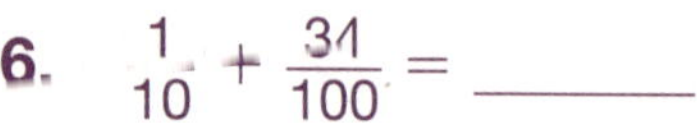

6. $\frac{1}{10} + \frac{34}{100} =$ ______

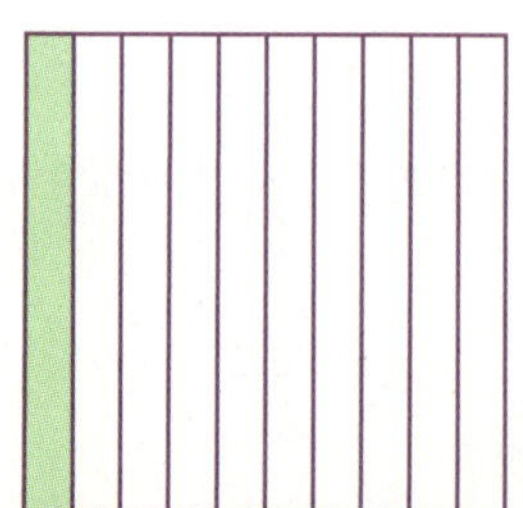

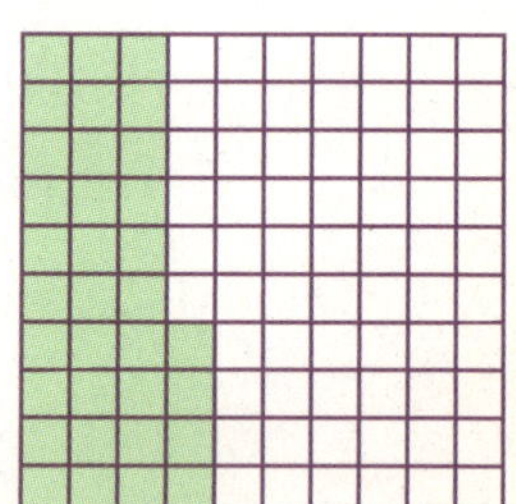

7. $\frac{29}{100} + \frac{6}{10} =$ ______

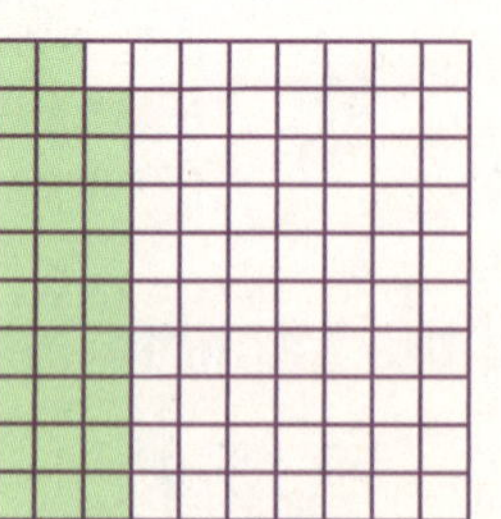

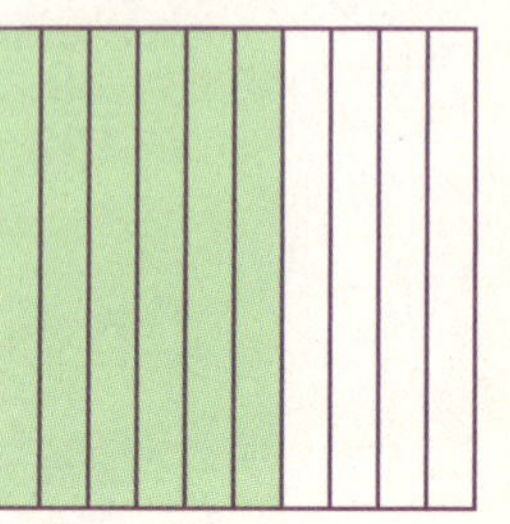

8. Brooke ran $\frac{7}{10}$ mile. Then she sprinted for $\frac{25}{100}$ mile. How far did Brooke run and sprint in all?

______

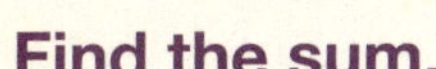

Find the sum.

9. $\frac{9}{10} + \frac{5}{100} =$ ______

10. $\frac{74}{100} + \frac{2}{10} =$ ______

11. $\frac{22}{100} + \frac{6}{10} =$ ______

12. $\frac{2}{10} + \frac{2}{100} =$ ______

13. $\frac{3}{10} + \frac{19}{100} =$ ______

14. $\frac{41}{100} + \frac{5}{10} =$ ______

15. $\frac{48}{100} + \frac{4}{10} =$ ______

16. $\frac{2}{10} + \frac{57}{100} =$ ______

17. $\frac{65}{100} + \frac{2}{10} =$ ______

18. $\frac{3}{100} + \frac{9}{10} =$ ______

19. $\frac{16}{100} + \frac{8}{10} =$ ______

20. $\frac{7}{10} + \frac{23}{100} =$ ______

Solve each problem.

21. Jeff lives $\frac{2}{10}$ kilometer from the park. The path around the park is $\frac{33}{100}$ kilometer long. Jeff walks to the park, walks around the park once, and then goes back home. How far does Jeff walk in all?

____

22. A community garden is on a 1-acre field. The garden is planted with tomatoes on $\frac{3}{10}$ of the field and corn on $\frac{1}{10}$ of the field. Squash are planted on $\frac{21}{100}$ of the field. What part of the field is planted with tomatoes, corn, and squash?

____

10 Compare Decimals

Key Words

is equal to
is greater than
is less than

You can use models to compare decimals as long as the wholes are both the same size. As the model shows, $0.5 \neq 0.5$ if the wholes being compared are not the same size.

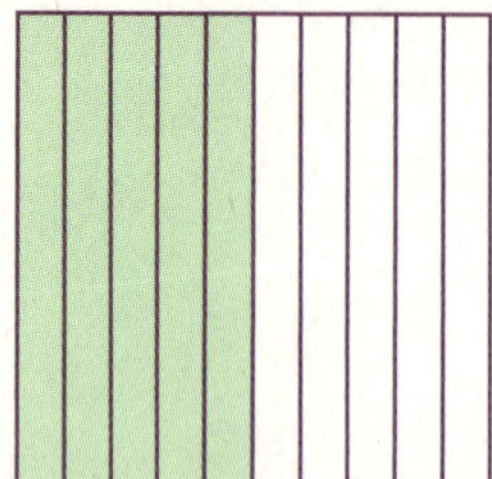

Use these symbols to compare decimals:

$>$ means **is greater than**

$<$ means **is less than**

$=$ means **is equal to**

Example

Compare 0.5 and 0.38.

Use models to represent each decimal.
The wholes for both models must be the same size.

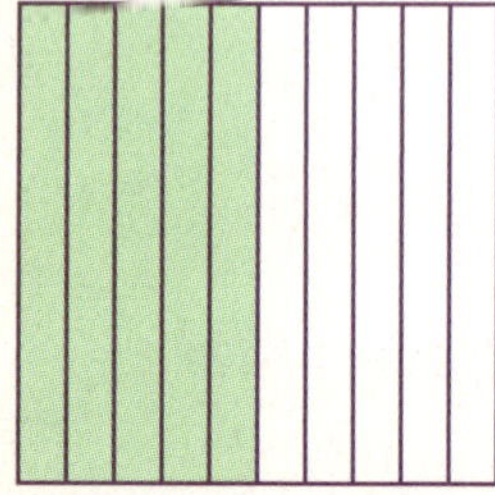

0.5

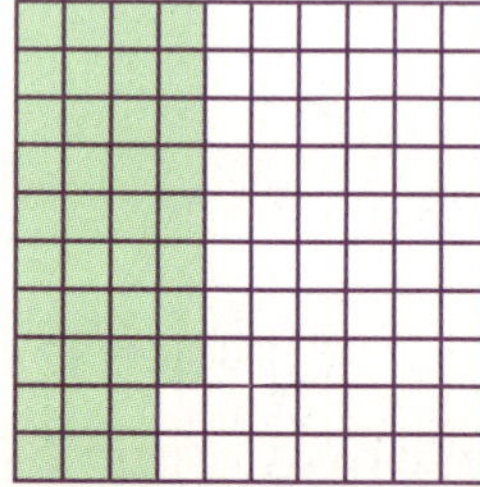

0.38

Use the models to compare the decimals.

The shaded part of the model for 0.5 is greater than the shaded part of the model for 0.38.

So 0.5 is the greater decimal.

$0.5 > 0.38$

JUSTIFY

To compare two decimals, the decimals must refer to the same whole. Why?

Guided Practice

1 Write >, <, or = to compare 0.40 and 0.4.

Step 1 Use models to represent each decimal.

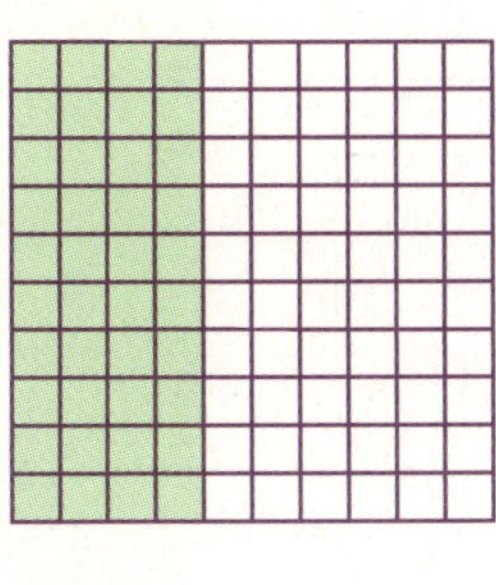

0.40

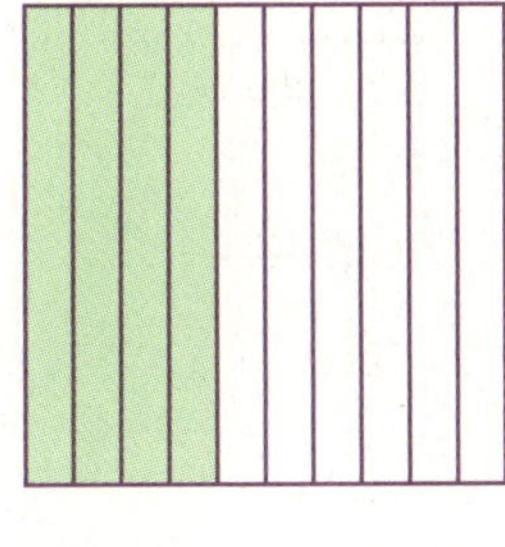

0.4

> **REMEMBER**
> The model for hundredths has 100 equal parts, and the model for tenths has 10 equal parts.

Step 2 Use the shaded parts of the models to compare the decimals.

The shaded part for 0.40 is __________ the shaded part for 0.4.

0.40 ◯ 0.4

2 Use >, <, or = to compare 0.29 and 0.52.

Step 1 Use models to represent each decimal.

Shade the models to show each decimal.

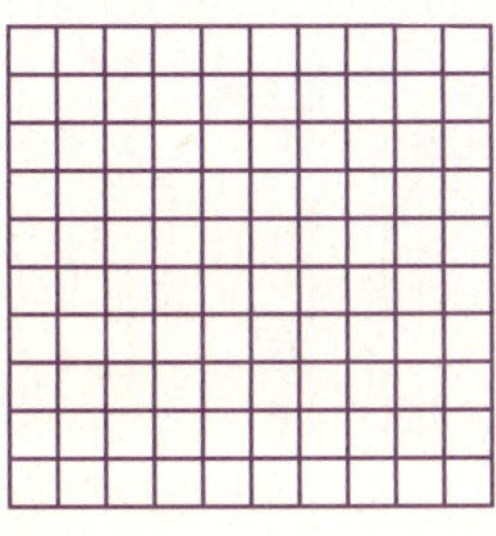

0.29

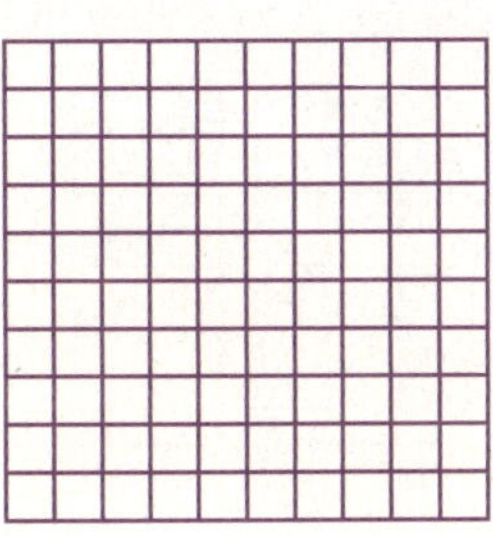

0.52

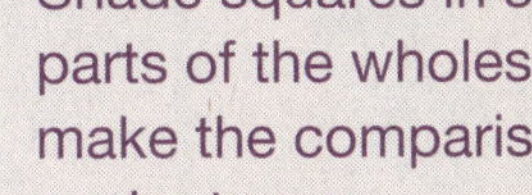

> Shade squares in similar parts of the wholes to make the comparison easier to see.

Step 2 Use the models to compare the decimals.

Which model has more squares shaded? ______

Which decimal is greater? ______

0.29 ◯ 0.52

> **REMEMBER**
> > means *is greater than*, and < means *is less than*.

Independent Practice

1. How can you use models to compare two decimals?

____

____

2. Why do models help in comparing decimals?

____

____

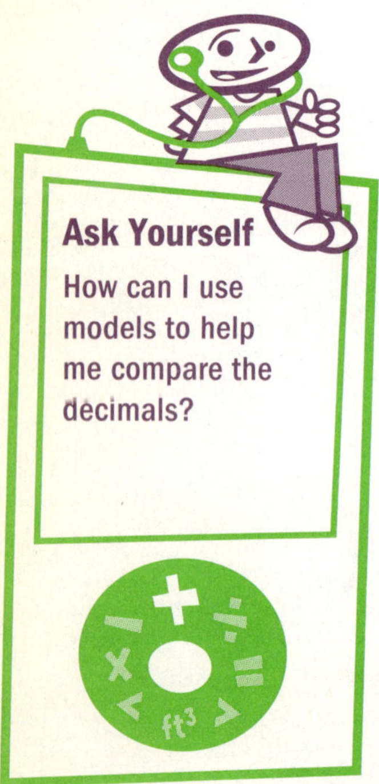

Compare. Write >, <, or =.

3. 0.3 ◯ 0.1

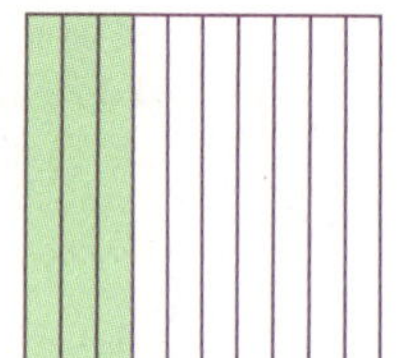

4. 0.46 ◯ 0.72

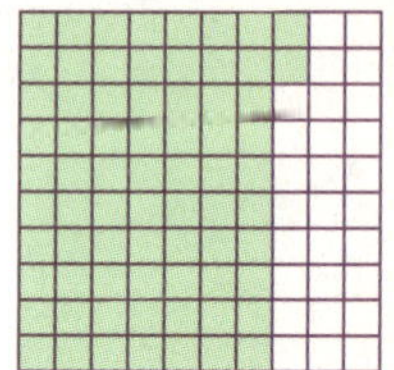

5. 0.54 ◯ 0.17

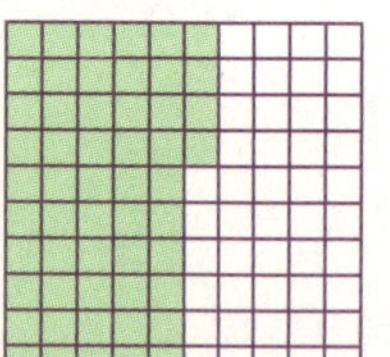

6. 0.8 ◯ 0.39

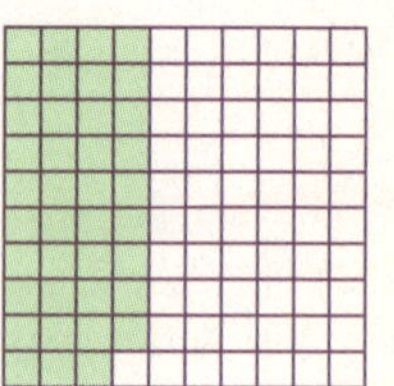

7. Rosa hiked 0.84 kilometer before taking a break. After the break, she hiked 0.79 kilometer. Which was greater, the distance hiked before the break or the distance hiked after the break?

____

Compare. Write >, <, or =.

8. 0.37 ◯ 0.31

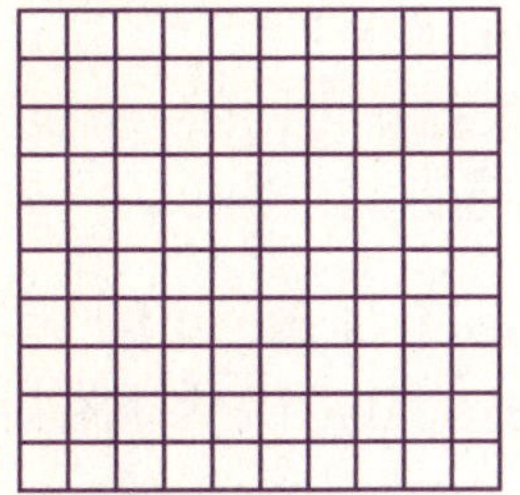
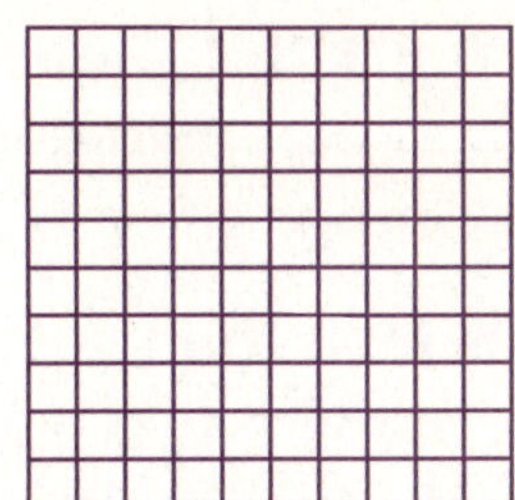

9. 0.2 ◯ 0.20

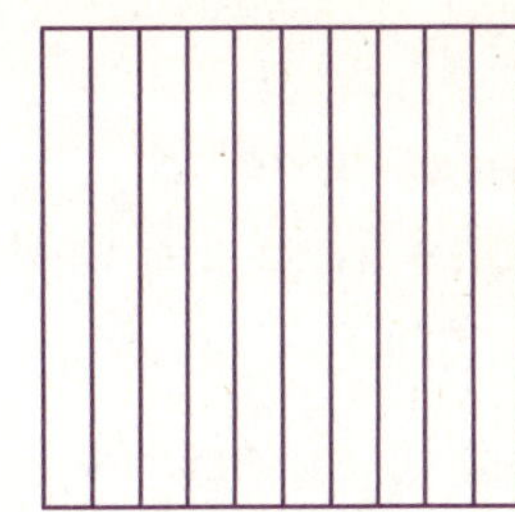

10. 0.52 ◯ 0.75

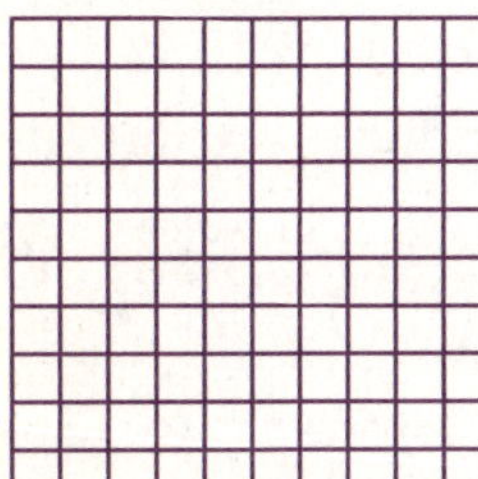
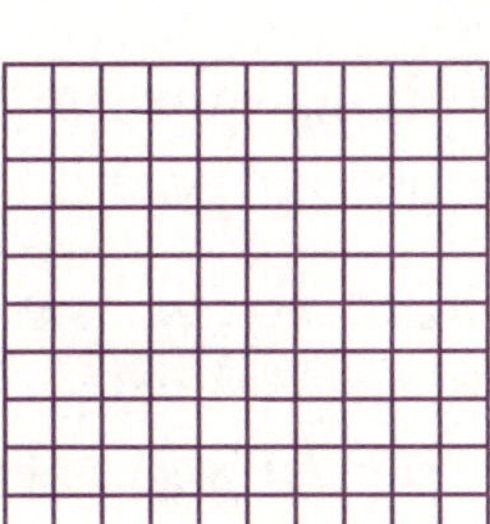

11. 0.6 ◯ 0.58

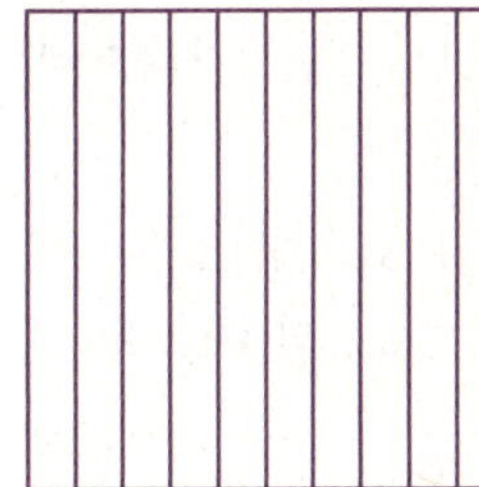
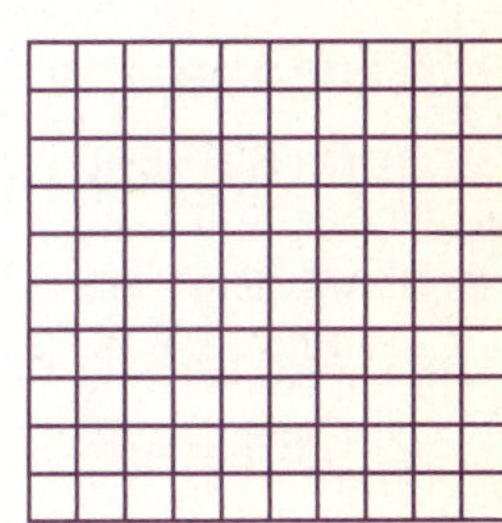

Write >, <, or = for each ◯.

12. 0.5 ◯ 0.36

13. 0.71 ◯ 0.45

14. 0.66 ◯ 0.6

Solve each problem.

15. A zucchini squash from Zoe's garden has a mass of 0.14 kilogram. An acorn squash from her garden has a mass of 0.62 kilogram. Which squash has the greater mass?

____

16. The trail to the base of a waterfall is 0.85 kilometer. The trail to the top of the waterfall is 0.49 kilometer. Which trail is shorter?

____

Glossary

addend a number to be added (Page 16)

decimal a number with one or more digits to the right of the decimal point (Page 32)

decimal point a symbol used to separate the ones place from the tenths place in a decimal number (Page 32)

denominator the part of a fraction that is written below the line; it tells the number of equal parts into which the whole or the group is divided (Page 4)

difference the answer to a subtraction problem (Page 20)

equivalent fractions fractions that name the same amount but have different numerators and denominators (Page 4)

factor one of the numbers multiplied to give a product (Page 28)

fraction a number that names equal parts of a whole or equal parts of a group (Page 4)

improper fraction a fraction with a numerator that is equal to or greater than its denominator (Pages 8 and 24)

is equal to a symbol (=) used to compare two numbers to show that they have the same value (Pages 12 and 40)

is greater than a symbol (>) used to compare two numbers, with the greater number given first (Pages 12 and 40)

is less than a symbol (<) used to compare two numbers, with the lesser number given first (Pages 12 and 40)

like denominators denominators that are the same (Page 16)

mixed number a number with a whole number part and a fraction part (Page 8)

numerator the part of a fraction that is written above the line; it tells how many equal parts are represented by a fraction (Page 4)

product the answer in a multiplication problem (Page 28)

sum the answer to an addition problem (Page 16)

unit fraction a fraction with a numerator of 1 (Page 16)

Math Tools: Fraction Strips

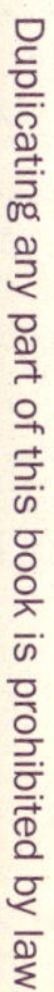

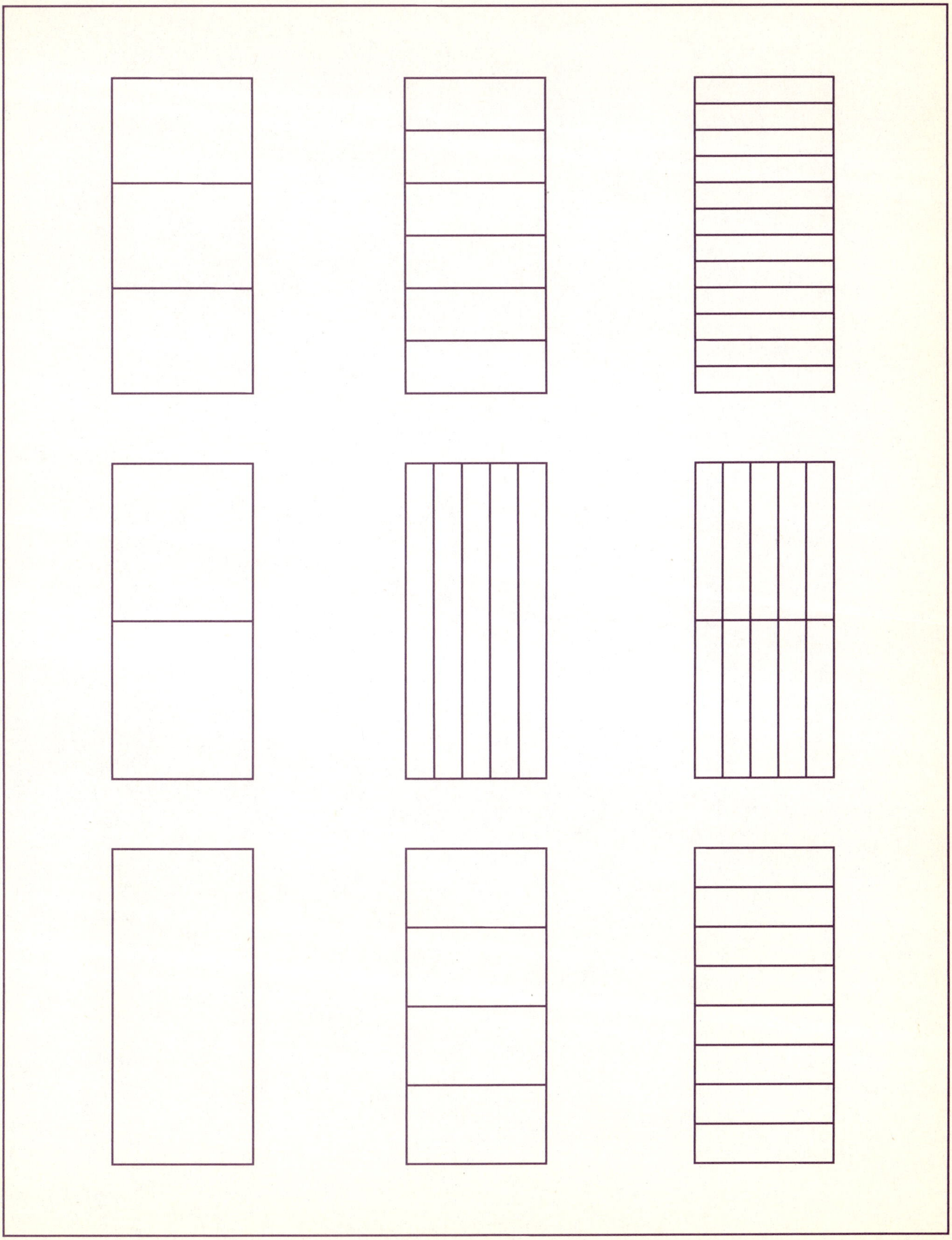

Math Tools: Number Lines

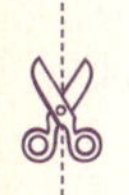

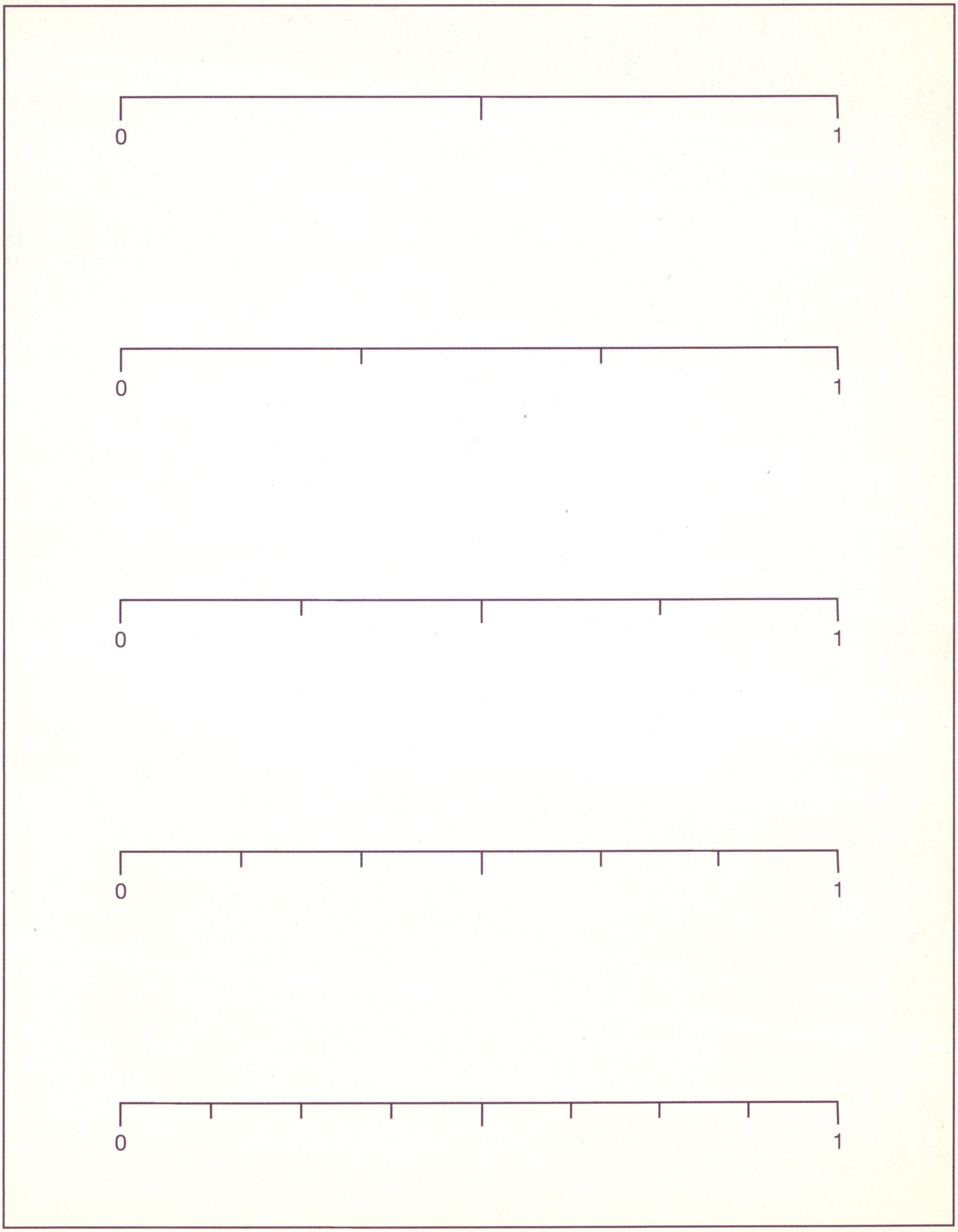

Cut or tear carefully along this line.

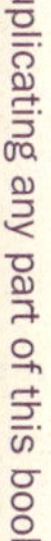

0 1

0 1

0 1

0 1

0 1